_Dan Green_

# The Preacher Joke Book

# The Preacher Joke Book

## Edited by Loyal Jones

Illustrated by Wendell E. Hall

*August House* / *Little Rock*
P U B L I S H E R S

Printed in the United States of America

10  9

LIBRARY OF CONGRESS CATALOGING-IN-PUBLICATION DATA

The Preacher joke book / edited by Loyal Jones ; illustrated by
Wendell E. Hall. — 1st ed.
    p. cm.
   ISBN 0-87483-088-5 (alk. paper)
   1. Clergy—Southern States—Humor. 2. Wit and humor—Religious
aspects—Christianity. 3. Southern States—Religious life and
customs—Humor. 4. Southern States—Social life and customs—Humor.
   I. Jones, Loyal, 1928-
PN6231.C5P74     1989
202'.07—dc20                   89-6612
                                          CIP

Cover illustration by Wendell E. Hall
Production artwork by Ira Hocut
Typography by Lettergraphics, Memphis, Tennessee
Design direction by Ted Parkhurst
Project direction by Hope Coulter

This book is printed on archival-quality paper which meets the
guidelines for performance and durability of the Committee on
Production Guidelines for Book Longevity of the Council on
Library Resources.

AUGUST HOUSE, INC.        PUBLISHERS        LITTLE ROCK

*For all of the believers
who have managed to keep a perspective on the
vagaries of life*

# Contents

# Preface

The ingredients for this book came from many sources. Some of the stories have been collected by the editor over a lifetime and the tellers are long forgotten. Some are from older printed or recorded sources now in the public domain. Many were contributed or suggested by friends and acquaintances. Their help is greatly appreciated.

Several people should be mentioned with particular gratitude. They are: Robert J. Higgs, of East Tennessee State University; Robert Cogswell, Tennessee state folklorist; Judge Sam J. Ervin, III, for permission to use some humor from his late father, Senator Sam J. Ervin, Jr.; Howard Dorgan, of Appalachian State University; Charles L. Perdue, of the University of Virginia; Robin P. Benke, of Clinch Valley College; Billy Wilson, of Berea, Kentucky; Justin Wilson, of French Settlement, Louisiana, and his publisher, Pelican Publishing Company of Gretna, Louisiana; Jo Lunsford Herron, for use of material from her late father, Bascom Lamar Lunsford; Bradley Kincaid, of Springfield, Ohio; Lee Morris, of Berea College; Saunders Guerrant, of Roanoke, Virginia; Carl Hurley, of Lexington, Kentucky; and George Goldtrap, of Nashville, Tennessee. Thanks go also to the University of Tennessee Press, the University of North Carolina Press, and the University of Georgia Press for permission to reprint several items. Others who contributed are mentioned elsewhere in the book. Know that you are appreciated.

Thanks also to Liz and Ted Parkhurst, who own and run August House and who conceived the idea for this book, to Hope Coulter, who edited it, to Wendell Hall, who splendidly illustrated it, and to Nancy, my wife, who spent some evenings alone because of it.

# Southern Religious Humor

The South is as diverse in religion as any other part of the country, perhaps more so. All of the mainline Protestant denominations are here, plus the Catholic and Jewish faiths, and also many locally autonomous Baptist and Pentecostal-Holiness groups and a good many that are hard to classify. Mainly, though, the South is under the heavy hand of John Calvin. The earlier churches, Presbyterian and Baptist, were strongly Calvinistic. Calvin preached that all things are foreordained and foreknown by God (predestination); that we cannot save ourselves from our natural fleshly state except by the grace of God; that if God has predestined us to be saved, we will be saved in spite of ourselves (and likewise that those predestined for hellfire cannot change where they're bound); that if we are among the elect, we shall persevere forever; and that we are in a fallen state and our only goodness comes from God. Such beliefs instill a profound humility, and this realization of our shortcomings is a prime source of humor in the South.

Such a set of beliefs ties in with the profound tragic view of life that pervades the South. Many writers have ascribed this view to the South's loss of the Civil War. That contributed, no doubt, but Calvinistic religion also has planted a sense of human failure, loss, and tragedy. Part of the tragedy (paraphrasing Reinhold Niebuhr) is that we see so clearly what we ought to be and do, and yet in striving we fail so consistently.

The Methodists, who were foils to Calvinists, soon followed the Baptists, Presbyterians, and Episcopalians and started the First Great Awakening in the 1730s along the frontier. Methodists believed in universal redemption, that is, that all people can be saved if they will but turn to God with a contrite heart and beg forgiveness for their sins. John Wesley would have nothing to do with what he considered to be the unfair and illogical doctrines of Calvin. As the late Senator Sam J. Irvin of North Carolina put it once, the early Calvinists believed that God knew everything that was to be, but the "free-will" folks like the Methodists believed that God was just as surprised as anybody else at what happened.

The effect of the First Great Awakening and then the Second, which began about 1800, was to convert a lot of folks from stern Calvinism to the more optimistic doctrine of free-will redemption. Some Baptists already had a strain of thought that allowed for universal redemption, but soon there were more kinds of free-will and "missionary" Baptists than you could shake a stick at, who felt that there was no time to waste in bringing the lost to salvation. Even among the Presbyterians, steeped in Calvinism, there was spawned a "New Light" group which embraced freewillism.

But free-will theology wasn't all that John Wesley had in mind for the Methodists. He believed that it is possi-

ble to achieve a state of holiness, to be sanctified or lifted above sin through a second act of grace. This belief really separated Methodists and their kind from the Calvinists. The latter believed that as long as we inhabit the flesh, we are heirs to the sins thereof. The former believed that if we avoid temptations, we can live a sinless life. At the tail end of the nineteenth century, there came the Pentecostal-Holiness movement whose leaders really took the "holiness" idea seriously, and they became more concerned with achieving a state of holiness than even the Methodists. They and most Methodists stressed avoiding temptatations, variously defined, including liquor, dancing, fiddle and banjo music, alluring clothing, makeup, movies, novels, and the opposite sex unless marriage was intended and imminent.

The old Calvinists were pretty tolerant of human weakness, and anyway, they didn't stress "conduct" or good works as a means to salvation. The perfectionists, on the other hand, did just that. They warned of the dangers of temptations, and soon put the quietus on revelry, ushering in the "Bluenose" era. Banjo players, such as Dock Boggs of Virginia, sold their banjos and fiddles or stored them in the attic when they "got religion." The redeemed gave up dancing and card playing. Preachers warned against all manner of temptations and thus made people feel guilty when involved in entertaining activities. Dancing was particularly condemned.

Do you know why Baptists can't make love standing up?
No, why?
God might think they were dancing.

But there is a gap between the desire to be perfect and the actuality. People do fail, and they suffer when they do, because there is a difference between our desires and our abilities. Situations created by the gap between our pretensions and our acts are prime sources of humor. Consider the fallen evangelists of recent times. They are of the perfectionistic persuasion. They pretended to be holy and righteous, in effect better than the rest of us. When they failed, the jokes started fast. Some were made up; others were old jokes recycled to fit the new situation. Examples:

Did you know that Bakker and Swaggart are starting a new magazine?
No. What are they going to call it?
*Repenthouse,* and it will have a Praymate of the Month.

Did you hear that Swaggart and Bakker are making a movie? They're going to call it *Children of the Looser God.*

We take a perverse pleasure in such jokes, some of which are as risqué as the evangelists' alleged acts, and they have spread rapidly throughout the country. They show us that those who pretended to be so much better than we are, are in fact no better, and this somehow makes us feel better about ourselves.

But the evangelists do not have to engage in vice to be the butt of jokes. Even though tent, radio, and, more recently, television evangelists are followed and even revered in the South, some of us, and perhaps most of us, at a certain level are uneasy about them. They have tended to be showy folks, bragging about having the biggest tent, or the most followers, or being on the most stations. They are not a modest lot, and this goes against the old Calvinist grain of the South. We may admire their style and opulence—as the peasants admired the kings—but at the same time we are uncomfortable about all of this and are always waiting for them to trip. In the old Southwest humor tradition of leveling out those who try to get above us, we make humor about the preachers. Examples:

Did you hear about Jerry Falwell's accident?
No, what happened?
He was out walking his pet duck and a motorboat ran over him.

Oral Roberts was so grateful for God's allowing him to raise the forty million dollars and not calling him home, that he decided he ought to do something to honor God. He thought about it and decided the most appropriate thing for him to do was to build a tomb for himself. Then he thought that it would be nice to have it in the Holy Land. So he called in one of his aides and asked him to go find an architect to draw up plans and then to scout out a suitable place to build the tomb. The aide did his bidding and returned with the plans and a picture of a nice site by an oasis in the Holy Land. The Rev. Mr. Roberts looked at them, quite pleased, and then asked, "How much is this going to cost?"
"Two million dollars," the aide replied.

"Oh no," said Roberts, "that's too much money for just three days' use."

This kind of joke that tends to level down the pretensions of the evangelists has a counterpart that applies to the "high church" people in the Catholic, Epsicopal, or even Presbyterian churches. One saying achieving this purpose and relating to the notion that we in the South are really Calvinists underneath (and thus mostly Baptists), goes like this:

A Methodist is a Baptist who's afraid of water, a Presbyterian is a Baptist who went to college, and an Episcopalian is a Baptist whose deals all worked out.

Another story—a favorite of the late Honorable Brooks Hays of Arkansas—shows disdain for the written, rather than the inspired, sermon:

The city preacher worked hard on his sermon most of the week and retyped it on Saturday night. But during the night his dog chewed it all up. He didn't notice until it was time to go to church. When he got in the pulpit, he said, "I had a nice sermon prepared for you this morning, but my dog chewed it up. I'm going to have to rely on the inspiration of the Lord today, but I promise to do better next Sunday."

A great deal of folk humor in the South ridicules ignorant or pompous preachers, or pious laypeople who pretend to be better than others. Some preposterous sermons, that were of the folk tradition or have entered it, are included in this collection. We accord preachers a place of respect at the same time that we ridicule them, especially the self-righteous ones. The South has been called "The Bible Belt" by people from elsewhere as a

term of derision. We really are a religious people, even though we have not always acted as our religion taught. Most of us are as decent, generous, and kind as people elsewhere, although in racial matters we white people have a lot for which to beg forgiveness. Most of us in the South are enthralled by religion, and yet we see humor in it. We aspire to do better than the ordinary, but we are often absurd, and we make jokes about that condition. Perhaps the jokes are as important as serious theological thought in defining God, our religion, and ourselves. Just as we are the only animals who can conceive of God, we are also the only ones who can laugh. There are many, like my friend Jack Higgs of Tennessee, who believe that somehow humor is close to the sacred. It helps us to keep objective, reminds us that we are fallible, that we are not the center of the universe, and that there is a whole lot that we do not know and still more that we don't understand. In the South, humor is a reflection of our belief that, considering all of this, the humble outlook is the only reasonable one. Our humor reinforces humility.

There is a lot of interfaith and interdenominational rivalry. Sometimes it is uncharitable and even mean. Many of the more conservative Protestant groups have said bad things about both Jews and Catholics, but those groups, on the other hand, have said things about the alleged ignorance of some of the Protestants. Most of the humor is pretty gentle, reflecting the view one person or group has of another. Here is a joke about a Catholic priest and a Jewish rabbi:

The largest Catholic church in the town was just across from the Jewish synagogue. Over time, a rivalry developed between the priest and the rabbi. If one planted shrubbery, so would the other. If one got a new suit, the other would get one too. One day, the priest's congregation bought him a new Cadillac. Soon the rabbi had a new Lincoln. The priest came out one morning, sprinkled the hood of the Cadillac with holy water, and blessed it. The rabbi came out with a pair of tin shears and cut an inch off the tailpipe of his Lincoln.

Each Protestant group tells stories on others. For example:

A lad in a Baptist family got the notion that he was going to become a preacher. So he would get up on a stump and preach to the chickens or whatever came by. He decided one day that he ought to practice the art of baptism. He looked around for suitable objects of the ceremony. Their old dog had had pups which had grown to a pretty good size. He rounded them up and took them down to the creek and began sousing them under with the appropriate words. He got down to the last one, which was the least sociable. When he picked it up, it growled and bit him, drawing some blood.

"Well," he said, "I'll just sprinkle you and let you go to hell."

A fairly well-known folksong, "Don't You Hear Jerusalem Mourn," has fun with several religious groups. This version is taken mostly from the singing of Cas Wallin of Sodom, North Carolina:

Here's a Baptist preacher, you can tell by his coat,
Don't you hear Jerusalem mourn?
Got a bottle in his pocket that he can't hardly tote,
Don't you hear Jerusalem mourn?

*Chorus:*
Don't you hear Jerusalem mourn?
Don't you hear Jerusalem mourn?
Thank God there's a heaven, and my soul's set free,
Don't you hear Jerusalem mourn?

Here's a Holiness preacher, he's all right . . .
But he'll roll and tumble and kick out the lights . . .

Here's a Methodist preacher, I do know . . .
He'll never let a chicken get big enough to crow . . .

Here's a Free-Will Baptist, he's okay . . .
He's got to get saved every other day . . .

Here's a Presbyterian, they're so proud . . . .
His neck's so stiff he can't hardly bow . . .

There's a Campbellite preacher down the way . . .
He has to get baptized every other day . . .

Here's a Catholic priest, he'll jingle his bell . . .
He'll take ten dollars and pray you out of hell . . .

There is a rich folklore in the South—including ballads,

songs, tales, and riddles. Many of these touch on religion. Several folktales have been included that relate to preachers and to a character not mentioned too often in the mainline churches but who is still vigorously alive in the chuches of the common folk, namely the Devil—Old Scratch. Old Horny. The Evil One. Since one function of folktales is to give us, who are often dumb and feckless, a vicarious sense of dealing with powers and principalities, these help us to believe that we can put even the Devil in his place.

The South is not the exclusive province of the religion described here, and the South is changing, becoming more like the rest of the nation. But underneath, the South has a distinctive outlook that the careful observer notices. Religion is pervasive in both black and white cultures. There is a personalism that is rare—except in rural areas—elsewhere in the country. The concept of the human condition includes the sense of tragedy mentioned earlier and engenders a fundamental modesty or humility. Those who are alert to social and cultural values know when they are in the South and not elsewhere. It is still a place where people laugh at themselves—also at others, but mainly at themselves.

*Loyal Jones*
*Berea, Kentucky*

# Jokes

## Pioneers

It is said that the first missionaries to the Upland South were the Baptists. When trails were blazed, the Methodists came. The Presbyterians came with the first rough roads. The Episcopalians came with the first Pullman.

*Dr. Robert Johnstone*
BEREA, KENTUCKY

## Surrogate Prayer

Brother Gilbert was a Revolutionary War soldier who settled in Owsley County, Kentucky, and wanted to establish law and order there—as my father, Dr. Luther Ambrose, told the story. So he got elected sheriff of the county. However, he wasn't much impressed with the laws of the state, so he got himself elected to the legislature. He didn't think much of that body and its capacity for making better laws either, so he became a preacher. He was pious, lived an exemplary life, and tried to lead people into improving their ways.

Someone traded him a mule, however, that sorely tried his patience. It was balky and mean, would kick or run away with the plow. Therefore, he thought about the matter and hired the worst reprobate in the community to come and plow his corn. The sinner hitched up the mule, nearly getting killed in the process, and then the mule balked, wouldn't do a thing. The reprobate wound up and addressed the mule with vile and disgusting invective. The mule stepped out smartly, and he plowed a row of corn. When he returned to the end of the row, he asked Brother Gilbert if they could pray. The preacher was pleased with this overture, and they both knelt. The reprobate prayed, "Lord, chalk those words up to Brother Gilbert. Amen."

*Martin Ambrose*
**BEREA, KENTUCKY, AND SAN MARINO, CALIFOR-NIA**

## Kinfolks

A preacher was walking down the road and came to a dead mule that had been hit by a truck. He recognized the mule and walked to the owner's house to tell him about it and to express his regrets. The owner of the mule said, "Well, it is the custom here for the persons who find something like that to take responsibility for burying it."

"All right," the preacher said, "but I just thought I'd notify the next of kin."

*Martin Ambrose*

## Likes Big Days

There was this Methodist preacher in the early days of Kentucky who got lost on Cumberland Mountain. There was a house about every twelve or fourteen miles apart. He found a path and followed it until he came to a little log house, and he hollered. There was a little woman stuck her head out the door, and he spoke to her, said, "I'm lost. Could you tell me which way to go?"

She said, "You go out here about a hill and a half until you come to the bear pen, turn left and it will take you over in there som'eres or other."

He saw right then that he was into it. He said, "Where's your husband?"

She said, "He's a-huntin.'"

"My lands-a-livin'," he said. "Huntin' here on the Sabbath day? Doesn't he know that there's coming an end, that people ought to live better than that—out a-huntin' on the Sabbath day? Doesn't he know that there's going to be a Judgment Day?"

She said, "Now if you see him anywhere, don't tell him. He gets a gallon of whiskey and goes to ever' big day he hears about. Don't you tell him. He's mean. He'll get drunk and tear that Judgment Day all to pieces!"

Well, he said, "I don't know what to think. Do you have any Methodist converts around here?"

She said, "I don't know. My old man kills a lot of varmints, skins them and tacks their hides up on the back of the house. You can go look."

He said, "What time is it?"

Back then they didn't have any timepieces. She stepped back and let the sun shine on the puncheon floor, said, "It's a puncheon-and-a-half till twelve."

"Lady," he said. "You're weak, aren't you."

She said, "If you'd had the diarrhea as long as I have, you'd be weak too."

So he never could get no sense out of her, and he said, "You're living in darkness."

"Yes," she said, "But John's a-goin' to put me a window in here."

So the preacher went on.

*Virgil Anderson*
ROCKY BRANCH, KEN-
TUCKY

## Bleak Prospects

Me and my father were making a crop back in the 1930s. He was working on one side of the hill, and I was on the other. I started singing, "Will There Be Any Stars in My Crown?" and I heard him singing, "No, Not One."

*Virgil Anderson*

## Who's First

The old Baptist preacher was warming to his subject about the advantageous position of Baptists in the scheme of things connected to the hereafter.

"Now who is going to be the first into heaven?" he asked rhetorically. "I'll tell you who is going to be first. It is going to be the Baptists."

A visiting Presbyterian lady was offended by this assertion, and she rose to debate.

"I can't accept that," she said. "I've been taught that the Presbyterians will be first."

"You are probably right, sister," the preacher responded. "The Scriptures say, 'The dead in Christ shall rise first.'"

*Loyal Jones*

## Absolution

The new priest from up north was assigned to the south Georgia peanut-growing country, and he had some difficulty in understanding the ways of the South. One day he was in the confessional booth, and three boys came to confess. He asked the first two how they had sinned and they answered in turn, "We've been throwing peanuts in the river."

He didn't understand how that was a sin, but he didn't want to ask, so he absolved them, and they left. However, after he had absolved the third boy of some minor infraction, he asked, "Why is it bad to throw peanuts in the river?"

"I'm Peanuts," said the boy.

*Rev. Charles Murray*
BEREA, KENTUCKY

## Apostolic Style

The old lady went to church and heard a young minister preach. When she got out, somebody asked her what she thought of his preaching.

She said, "He spoke in true apostolic style. He took a text and went everywhere preaching the gospel."

*Sen. Sam J. Ervin, Jr.*
MORGANTON, NORTH
CAROLINA

## Thank Heaven

This teacher went into her classroom about fifteen minutes before the class was supposed to begin and caught a bunch of boys down in a huddle on their knees in the corner of the room. She demanded of them what they were doing, and one of them hollered back, "We are shooting craps."

She said, "That's all right. I was afraid you were praying."

Sen. Sam J. Ervin, Jr.

## *Guaranteed*

The priest had come home with the family of new converts for dinner. He was received cordially by all but the small daughter in the family, who stared at him unblinkingly throughout the meal. The priest, somewhat uncomfortable, tried to put the little girl at ease.

"Is it my collar you are staring at?" he asked, taking it off and holding it up. When he did so he saw the cleaning instructions on the inside of the collar, and to make conversation, he asked, "Do you know what it says here?"

"Yes," responded the little girl. "It says, 'Kills fleas for six months.'"

**Buddy Westbrook**
LONDON, KENTUCKY

## *Too Much Fuel*

Back in the old days some of the Calvinist preachers were not adverse to a nip of whiskey now and then. This young preacher was nervous about preaching his first full-fledged sermon, so the older preacher told him that he sometimes took a little drink to calm his nerves and to get his mind stimulated. So he put a glass of clear liquor on the pulpit for the young preacher to use, as if it were water. However, the young preacher was so nervous, he drained the glass and then proceeded with his sermon. When he was finished, he mopped his brow and asked the older preacher how he had done.

"Well," said the old preacher, "in the first place, you

26

should have finished by noon, not two-thirty, and second, David slew the giant. He didn't stomp hell out of him!"

*Ralph Gabbard*
LEXINGTON, KENTUCKY

## Wrong Time

Years ago when the Northern Lights were especially bright, a young man went out late one night, saw them, and thought it was the end of time. He rushed down through the community, trying to wake people up. He came to the house of an old man, started pounding on his door, yelling, "Get up! The Day of Judgment has come!"

The old man yelled back, "Go back to bed. Who ever heard of the Day of Judgment coming in the middle of the night?"

*Hilde Capps*
BEREA, KENTUCKY

## Not Fit For A Dog

A young preacher was invited into a church to preach a trial sermon, with the understanding that he might be hired as pastor. He liked the looks of the church, and he liked the people. Everything was fine at the beginning of the service, with the hymns and the prayer. As the young preacher mounted the pulpit, however, an old man came in, followed by a huge Redbone hound. He sat down on the front row, and his dog plopped down beside him. The young preacher thought this was unusual, but he read his text and launched his sermon, at which point the hound let out a huge yawn with a yip at the end. This interrupted the preacher, but he began again. The dog began to scratch a flea, his leg whacking the floor with each lick, and the preacher stopped again and asked if someone would take the dog outside. Neither the old man nor anyone else moved, so the preacher started in again. The dog let out a growl and a deep bark, disturbed at something he heard outside. Again the preacher stopped and again asked if someone would take the dog outside. When no one responded, he got down from the pulpit, took the dog by the collar, led him outside, and closed the door behind him. Returning to the pulpit, he preached a pretty good sermon.

After the service he asked the deacon who was head of the pulpit committee how he had done.

"Well," the deacon said. "You preached a right good sermon. I believe you're all right there, but you really shouldn't have taken Old Man Johnson's dog out. I know the dog disturbed you, but you know, Mr. Johnson is a faithful member of this church, and he's on our pulpit committee. He always brings his dog to church. He loves that dog, and we're used to it, and it don't bother us to have him here. I think that you ought to apologize to Mr. Johnson for throwing his dog out like that. I believe you better do that."

So the young preacher approached the old man outside and said, "I'm sorry I put your dog out. The deacon here told me how much you think of your dog and how you always bring him to church. I'm real sorry that I did that, and I hope you'll accept my apology."

"Oh, that's all right," the old man said. "I wouldn't have wanted my dog to hear that sermon anyhow."

*Dr. Lee Morris*
BEREA, KENTUCKY

## Needed Fuel

A preacher stayed with a farm couple on a Saturday night before preaching on Sunday. The wife got up early to cook a huge breakfast, and then called her husband and the preacher. The preacher came down but said, "I never eat before I preach."

The man and woman ate, and then the woman and the preacher went on to church. The man stayed home. When his wife returned after the service, he asked how the sermon was.

"He could have et first," the woman said.

*Loyal Jones*

## No Reflection on You

A man got up in the middle of the pastor's sermon and walked out. After church, his embarrassed wife sought to explain to the preacher.

"I hope you don't think he disagreed with what you said. He just has a tendency to walk in his sleep."

**Dr. Charles S. Webster**
**NAPLES, FLORIDA**

## Compensating Factors

A young minister was courting two women, one tall, shapely, beautiful, but not too much inclined to be a preacher's wife. The other was somewhat homely but was a wonderful organist, choir leader, and soloist. He sought the counsel of an older pastor. Listening to descriptions of the two women, he offered his advice.

"Marry the one with the musical talent. She'll be a fine partner for you in your ministry."

So the young preacher married this woman. On their wedding night, he got into bed. After a while she came out of the bathroom in a see-through gown and with her hair in curlers. He stared at her and said,

"Sing, Myrtle, sing."

*Loyal Jones*

## Puny
*Question:* "Are you a Methodist?"
*Answer:* "No, I've been sick."

*Loyal Jones*

## Backslider
There was this sinner who would get religion every time they had a revival meeting, and then he would backslide until the next revival. After about six times at the baptizing hole, the preacher put him under, raised him up, and said,

"You've been baptized so much that the fish know you by your first name."

*Russell Hensley*
BEREA, KENTUCKY

## Watch the Metaphor
The preacher was waxing eloquent at the funeral of a departed church member. He concluded by saying,

*31*

"What we have here is just the shell. The nut has gone on."

*Rev. Herbert Banks*
UZ, KENTUCKY

## Fair's Fair

A bunch of loafers were sitting around a country store discussing the selection of a new pope, which was then in process. One old fellow listened for a while and then said, "Well, I think the Catholics have had it long enough. I hope a Baptist gets it this time."

*Wilma Dykeman*
NEWPORT, TENNESSEE

## Good Excuse

Two fishermen were out in a boat on a Sunday morning, not having too much luck. One of them got to thinking about what they were doing and said, "I feel bad being out here fishing when I ought to be in church."

"Yes, I know how you feel," the other said, "but I couldn't have gone anyway. My wife's sick."

*Loyal Jones*

## A Believer

This fellow said that his grandmother was so hooked on the TV soap operas that when one of the characters got sick, she'd stand up in church and ask for prayers for them.

*Dr. Charles L. Cox*
OAK RIDGE, TENNESSEE

## Forgot to Ask

A woman called on the Presbyterian minister and asked him if he would preach a funeral for her dog who had died.

"I can't do that, ma'am," he said. "Why don't you try the Baptist preacher?"

"All right," she said, "but can you give me some advice. How much should I pay him—three hundred dollars or four hundred dollars?"

"Hold on," he said, "I didn't know your dog was a Presbyterian."

*Guy Wesley*
LOUISVILLE, KENTUCKY

## Long, Long Wait

A couple who had been courting for ten or fifteen years got killed in a car accident, and when they arrived at the gates of heaven they informed St. Peter that they regretted not getting married on earth and asked if they could get married in heaven.

"Well, you'll have to wait a while," said St. Peter.

So they waited a year and went back to see St. Peter again, said, "We really want to get married, and we don't understand why we have to wait."

"You'll have to wait a while longer," said the venerable saint.

They waited two years and then went back again and said, "We can't understand why you are putting us off. We've come for an explanation."

St. Peter scratched his head and hemmed and hawed, said, "Well, it's like this. We're waiting for a preacher, but we expect one soon." Then he said, "It's a good thing you want to get married and not get a divorce. We don't know whether or not we'll ever get a lawyer!"

*Rev. Tim Jesson*
PRESTONSBURG, KEN-
TUCKY

## Just Pick Up the Phone

A preacher walking along the street encountered a woman of the night proposing to ply her trade. He was shocked, told her he was a man of the cloth, and proceeded to lecture her on the errors of her ways. Proceeding on home, he was much troubled by the encounter, and he worried and prayed about her far into the night.

The next morning he was walking down the same street when he saw the woman again.

"Madam," he said, "I prayed for you last night."

"Well, Reverend, you didn't have to do that. If you'd telephoned, I'd have come right over."

*Loyal Jones*

## Worth Knowing

The preacher was teaching the adult Sunday school class, and he was enthusiastically telling about Solomon and his seven hundred wives and three hundred concubines, and then for good measure, he threw in that he "fed them on ambrosia."

"Never mind that," said a little man who was intrigued with the story, "what did *he* eat?"

*Loyal Jones*

## A Mystery

A man stayed home while his wife went to church. When she returned, he inquired about the sermon. She said it was okay.

"Well what did the preacher preach about?" he persisted.

"I don't know," she said, "he never did say."

*Loyal Jones*

## A Candid Testimony

Many years ago there was a custom in a section of my country, known as the South Mountains, to hold religious meetings at which the oldest members of the congregation were called upon to stand up and pubicly testify to their religious experiences. On one occasion they were holding such a meeting in one of the churches, and old Uncle Ephriam Swink, a South Mountaineer, whose body was all bent and distorted with arthritis, was present. All of the other members of the congregation except Uncle Ephriam arose and gave testimony to their religious experiences. Uncle Ephriam kept his seat. Thereupon, the moderator said, "Brother Ephriam, suppose you tell us what the Lord has done for you."

Uncle Ephriam arose, with his bent and distorted body, and said, "Brother, he has mighty nigh ruint me."

*Sen. Sam J. Ervin, Jr.*
MORGANTON, NORTH
CAROLINA

## Decision

A cock fighter got religion, and a friend asked him how that came about. He replied, "Well, one night the Lord spoke to me and said, 'It's me or the chickens.'"

*Patsy Sims*
WASHINGTON, D.C.

## Topknots

In North Carolina about seventy-five years ago, the women had a habit of wearing their hair in topknots. This preacher deplored the habit. As a consequence, he preached a rip-snorting sermon one Sunday on the text "Topknot Come Down." At the conclusion of his sermon an irate woman, wearing a very pronounced topknot, told the preacher that no such text could be found in the Bible. The preacher thereupon opened the Scriptures to the seventeenth verse of the twenty-fourth chapter of Matthew and pointed to the words "Let him which is on the housetop not come down to take anything out of the house."

*Sen. Sam J. Ervin, Jr.*
MORGANTON, NORTH
CAROLINA

## Not That Drunk

John Watts took a notion that he was called to preach. John was skilled in the science of a bricklayer, but was sadly deficient in the art of an exhorter. He was nevertheless expounding the scriptures in a small rural church one Sunday, when Job Hicks, who had partaken too freely of Burke County corn, happened to stagger by. Upon seeing John in the pulpit, Job entered the church, dragged John to the door, and threw him out upon the ground. When Job Hicks was called to the bar to be sentenced for his offense, Judge Robinson, the presiding judge, remarked to him in a stern tone of voice, "Mr. Hicks, when you were guilty of this unseemly conduct on the Sabbath Day, you must have been so intoxicated as not to realize what you were doing."

Job made this response to His Honor: "Well, Judge, I had had several drinks. But I would not want Your Honor to think I was so drunk I could stand by and see the Word of the Lord being mummicked up like that without doing something about it."

*Sen. Sam J. Ervin, Jr.*

## *Firm Knowledge*

There was a Presbyterian and a Methodist down in North Carolina who got to arguing about the Presbyterian doctrine of predestination, and like all religious arguments the longer it lasted the more wrathful the participants became. Finally the Methodist said, "Well, I will admit there may be something to the doctrine of predestination. I think Presbyterians are predestined to go to hell."

Then the Presbyterian said to the Methodist, "Well, I would rather be a Presbyterian and know I am going to hell than to be a Methodist and not know where in the hell I am going."

*Sen. Sam J. Ervin, Jr.*

## *A Real Squeeze*

The strong man at the circus was demonstrating his strength by taking a green stick and squeezing the sap out of it. When he had squeezed out several drops, he asked if anyone from the audience would like to try, and

a frail-looking little lady came forward, took the stick in both hands, and squeezed. To the amazement of the strong man, a rivulet of sap ran down over her knuckles.

"Who are you, anyhow, lady?" he asked.

"Oh, I'm just the treasurer at a Methodist church," she replied.

*Bob Sears*
SOMERSET, KENTUCKY

## Relative Faithfulness

Three men died and went to heaven. St. Peter met them at the front gate and said, "Heaven is a great big place, and we'll assign you a vehicle to get around in based on how faithful you were to your wives."

So he gave the first man a Cadillac, the second one a Chevrolet, and the third a motorcycle. The one who got the motorcycle was somewhat disappointed, but he figured that it was fair, based on his degree of faithfulness. He went driving down one of the streets of heaven, and he saw the man who got the Cadillac parked on the curb, and he was crying loudly. He stopped and asked, "What in the world are you crying about? You got the Cadillac."

"I know," said the man, "and I just saw my wife go by on a skateboard."

*Jane Winstead*
SNEEDVILLE, TENNESSEE

## Going to See the Pope

A barber in a small Tennessee town was a well-known pessimist. No matter what was said to him, he would find something negative to say about it. One day a fellow went in to get a haircut, and while the barber was working on him he said, "Well, I've decided to do something different this year for my vacation. I'm going to go to Rome and see the pope."

"You don't want to do that," the barber said. "Rome is a dirty city and not safe to be in, and anyway, you can't see the Pope. Why, when he speaks out there on that balcony, there'll be a hundred thousand people there to hear him. There's no way you could get in to see him."

That fellow left, didn't say anything more, but in a couple of months he came back in to get his hair cut again, and the barber asked sarcastically, "Did you go to Rome and see the pope?"

"Yes, I did," the man said, "but you were wrong about Rome. It is a beautiful city and just as safe as it is here. You were right about one thing, though. There were at least a hundred thousand people out there when the pope spoke from his balcony, and I was right there in the middle of them. I thought, 'I'll never get to see the pope with this many people here,' but just when he finished talking, this fellow came up behind me and said that the pope wanted me to come to see him. So, I went with him and saw the pope, knelt down in front of him, kissed his ring, and he blessed me."

"Oh, come on," said the barber. "I don't believe a word of that. Why would he pick you out of all of those people?"

"Well, I thought of that," said the man, "and I asked him, 'Mr. Pope, why did you pick me out of all of those people?' and he said, 'When I looked out over the crowd, you had the worst haircut I ever saw, and I just wanted to advise you to find a new barber.'"

*Carl McMurry*
TAZEWELL, TENNESSEE

## Cleaned Up Good

There was a poor family lived in this town, and some-one brought them to the attention of the Baptist minis-ter. They said they would like to go to church but that they didn't have any dress clothes to wear. So the preacher put out word to his congregation that he needed clothing for the family, got some real nice chil-dren's clothes and some for the mother and father too, real nice clothing. He took it down to the family, and they seemed grateful. The preacher invited them to come to church next Sunday, and they said they would. Sunday came, though, and the family didn't come, so the preacher went down to see them on Monday, said, "You promised me that you would come down to our church Sunday."

"Yes, I know we did," the man of the house said, "but when we got all cleaned up and got on those nice clothes you brought, we looked so good we decided to go to the Episcopal church."

*Dr. Robert Johnstone*
BEREA, KENTUCKY

## With My Own Eyes

One Baptist to another: "Do you believe in infant baptism?"

Answer: "Believe in it? I've actually seen it done!"

*Rev. Will D. Campbell*
MT. JULIET, TENNESSEE

## Quaker Revenge

A gentle Quaker farmer had a particularly stubborn and uncooperative mule who tried his patience daily. One day, after a trying time plowing corn, the Quaker addressed his mule: "Thou knowest that I cannot strike thee, and thou knowest that I cannot curse thee, but what thou doesn't know is that I can sell thee to a Baptist and he will do to thee what I cannot."

*Loyal Jones*

## *Body and Soul*

It was the custom to have some new preacher come at revival time every summer to infuse the meetings with a new outlook on the ways of the Lord. Like a tonic to the spirit, you might say, and maybe somebody would draw bigger crowds. One year, they called in a man from someplace far off like West Virginia. He had the reputation of being a fire-and-brimstone evangelist, a real Bible-thumper who could get folks so worked up they'd be shouting in the aisles and swarming to the altar in droves. He turned out to be a feisty-looking man, small-ish, one of those dark and wiry kinds with such an inner fervor that he could light a match just by looking at it. He had a real singing voice, too, and led all the hymns, marking the beat by thumping his fist on his Bible, shouting the words out to the congregation. It was a glorious time at his first Saturday night meeting, and he worked everybody up into a real frenzy with hair-raising threats about the wages of sin and the terrible vengeance the Lord called down on the fornicators, prevaricators, and adulterers. Of course, everybody clamored to have him staying at their houses, and his Sunday dinner invitations were too many to count.

It so happened that he went home with one of the elder deacons who had put five dollars in the offering the first night. Now, this deacon was a God-fearing man, but he was old, and a few years back had married a much younger woman. She served up a fine dinner after the Sunday morning meeting, a regular feast, and she kept giving all the choice pieces of meat and the best biscuits to the new preacher, ladling his gravy for him and leaning over his chair to make sure his plate was full enough. When it was time to go to the evening service, her husband left early to make a church-related visit to one of the neighbors. She said she'd be along later, after she finished the chores.

As the regular preacher and the new preacher walked along the road to the church house, they discussed the fine feast they'd had and the merits of their hostess.

"She's a woman of the true Christian spirit," the regular preacher said. "I guess she loves the Lord a lot, with all that attention she was paying you. Leaning over you that way. Looking out for your needs and feeding the body as well as the—"

"Here, hold my coat," the new preacher said, turning around in the road. "I'll be there for services atter a while."

*Betty Payne James*
*as told by her father,*
*John Payne*
DISPUTANTA, KENTUCKY

## Shall We Gather . . .

Aunt Kate Simpson's youngest son, Roland, was not all that bright. As a matter of fact, he was downright slow in his thinking. After he failed the primer in school for about six years in a row, they didn't make him go to school any more. And even when he was almost a full-grown man, he followed Aunt Kate around wherever she went, shuffling along behind her like a big mule.

One year at revival time, Aunt Kate rededicated her life to the Lord. The preacher was fairly new and filled with the fervor of washing everybody in the Blood of the Lamb, so he called all the old Christians as well as the new ones to be reconsecrated by baptism in the waters of Clear Creek. All the folks to be baptized gathered on a Sunday afternoon with all of their relatives and kin, neighbors and friends, alongside the banks of the big open space of murkish green water down on the edge of O.M. Payne's cornfield. Everybody sang "Shall We Gather at the River" and "Are You Washed in the Blood of the Lamb," the preacher prayed a good long prayer, and the baptizing got underway.

One at a time, he called them forward into the water where he stood waist-deep, waiting. When it was Aunt Kate's turn to go down into the water, Roland kept right behind her, all the way in, up to his hips. The preacher prayed a little prayer, positioned Aunt Kate's hands just right over her mouth and nose with the handkerchief she was clutching, and doused her under. She came up real graceful-like, not even sputtering. As she started to the other creekbank, with Roland right behind her, the preacher reached out for Roland, thinking he must be next. He grabbed him with a good tight grip and plunged him down out of sight under the water. Roland fought and bucked and kicked great waves in every direction, churning the water like some kind of machine. When he was finally able to fight loose of the preacher and get away to the far creekbank, he blew water out of his mouth and nose and shook himself all over like a dog. Then he checked the pockets of his overalls, taking out the contents and fumbling through them.

"Well, boys!" he called to the crowd on the far bank. "Looks like I lost fifteen cents in the round."

*Betty Payne James*
*as told by John Payne*

## *Predestination*

All people would embrace Presbyterianism if they fully comprehended the doctrine of predestination. Although I cannot explain it in theological terms, I can make its real significance plain by relating a story, which may be apocryphal, about Major Robert Lewis Dabney, the Presbyterian minister who served as chief chaplain to Stonewall Jackson's command. . . .

According to the story, Major Dabney always preached to Jackson's men on predestination. He assured them that the Almighty had planned and predestined everything which was ever going to happen. Consequently, he further assured them, if they were predestined to be killed or wounded by a Yankee bullet, they could not possibly escape the bullet; on the contrary, if they were not predestined to be killed or wounded by a Yankee bullet, no Yankee bullet could harm them. He added that for these reasons they ought to maintain absolute serenity in the midst of the hottest battle.

One day a skirmish occurred while Major Dabney was visiting the front. As the Yankee bullets began to kick up dust spots around him, the major ran as fast as he could and jumped behind a tree.

A Confederate private, who had already taken refuge behind the tree, remarked, "Major Dabney, you don't practice what you preach?"

The major inquired, "What do you mean, my good man?"

The Confederate soldier replied, "You're always telling us that everything that's going to happen has been planned and predestined by the Almighty; that we can't possibly escape our predestined fate; and for that reason we should always be calm in battle. I noticed, however, that when the Yankee bullets began to kick up dust spots around you, you forgot about predestination, resorted to free will, undertook to save yourself, and ran and jumped behind this tree."

Major Dabney explained, "My good man, you do not fully understand the doctrine of predestination. You overlook two significant factors. The tree was predestined to be here, and I was predestined to run and jump behind it."

*Sen. Sam J. Ervin, Jr.*

In *Humor of a Country Lawyer* (Chapel Hill: University of North Carolina Press, 1983), pp. 82-83. Used by permission.

## Great Preachers

This preacher had delivered what he thought was a great sermon, and he was feeling good on the way home.

"How many great preachers do you think there are preaching today?" he asked his wife.

"One less than you think," she answered.

*Dr. Lee Morris*
BEREA, KENTUCKY

## Chain Preachers

The chief deacon of a church got a letter which read, "If you are tired of your preacher, send a copy of this letter to seven other churches who are probably tired of their preachers. Then ship your preacher to the church at the top of he list. Add the name of your church to the bottom. In thirty days, you will receive twenty-one hundred and seventy-eight preachers, and out of this many you ought to be able to choose one to suit you. Warning! One church broke the chain and got their old preacher back."

*Loyal Jones*

## Weak Vessel

There was this old boy who had been converted in every revival meeting that they had had, and every year they would have the same kind of prayer meeting at the altar, with everybody trying to "pray him through." After many years of it, they were all praying, "Lord, fill him with the Holy Ghost," but one old fellow was more of a realist. He said, "No use, Lord. He leaks."

*Edward Thomas*
**KEYSTONE, WEST VIR-
GINIA, AND
DELANO, CALIFORNIA**

## A Fellow Christian

A preacher went hunting out in the woods, heard a noise behind him, turned, and there was a big bear reared up on his hind legs. The preacher cocked his gun, aimed, and pulled the trigger. The gun only clicked, and the bear started toward him. He dropped to his knees and and prayed, "Lord, save me from this bear."

He looked up and the bear was still coming, and he prayed, "Lord, let this be a Christian bear."

He looked up again, and the bear was hunkered down praying, "Lord, bless this food for the needs of our body."

*Loyal Jones*

## Substitute Preacher

A popular preacher got sick on a Sunday morning, and he called a retired minister and asked if he would preach the service for him. The substitute agreed but felt inadequate in filling in for such a good preacher. When he entered the pulpit, he struggled for a metaphor that would express his humility in his task.

"I feel inadequate in taking the place of your minister this morning. He is such a good preacher and brings light just like the sunlight through a clean pane of glass. I, on the other hand, am like the piece of cardboard that you have seen substituted for the pane in a window."

He went on and preached a pretty good sermon. At the door afterwards, a good sister of the church gushed, "Preacher, you're no cardboard; you're a real pane."

*Loyal Jones*

## The Secret to Saintliness

The young new pastor was getting acquainted with his new flock, and eventually someone told him about Sister Johnson, who was too old to come to church anymore but who was a veritable saint, one who had worked long and hard in the service of the Lord. So he decided to make a call on her. She received him warmly.

Thinking there might be material for a sermon here, he asked her what the most important thing had been in her life. The old lady thought long and hard and then replied, "Well, taking everything into consideration, I guess it was my victuals."

*Hon. Brooks Hays*
LITTLE ROCK, ARKANSAS

## Vain Prayer

The preacher's little daughter noticed that her father always bowed his head for a minute before starting his sermon. One day she asked him why.

"Well, I'm asking the Lord to help me preach a good sermon."

"How come He doesn't do it?" she asked.

*Loyal Jones*

## Gabriel Tooting

A pious and excitable farmer was out plowing one day and thought he heard Gabriel tooting his horn. He threw down his plowlines and ran for the house calling for his wife. He was so excited that it took her a while to get him settled down. His two sons, who had been hoeing corn, came running to see what the commotion was and got there in time to hear their father say that he had heard Gabriel tooting his horn. The boys, not too religious, started laughing and making fun of their father. Their mother, protective of her husband, scolded them and said, "Maybe he did hear a toot or two."

*Gov. Bob Taylor*
NASHVILLE, TENNESSEE

## Saying

If all the people who sleep in church were laid end to end, they'd be more comfortable.

*Anonymous*

## Long Sermon

A preacher, known for long and boring sermons, had been into a particularly tedious one for nearly an hour, when he stopped to scold his congregation,

"I know you think my sermons are long, but I've got something important to impart to you. Now, I don't mind you looking at your watches while I'm preaching, but I want you to know that I resent you shaking them to see if they're still running."

*Loyal Jones*

## No Balance

A mother and her son, who weren't regular churchgoers, went to a new church for Sunday morning service. On their way home the mother asked her son what he thought of the service.

"Well, I liked the music, but I thought the commercial was too long."

*Loyal Jones*

## Emulation

A preacher on his deathbed summoned his doctor and his lawyer. They came, and he asked them to sit on either side of his bed and hold his hands. They sat thus for a long while until the doctor stirred and said, "You don't have long on this earth, Reverend. Better tell us why you asked us to come."

The old preacher stirred himself and wheezed, "Well, Jesus died between two thieves, and that's the way I want to go too."

*Dr. Louis Smith*
**BEREA, KENTUCKY**

## Broke

A good Methodist family dressed their little daughter up in an angel costume for Halloween trick-or-treating. They followed her discreetly as she went from door to door collecting cookies and candy in a large paper bag. Finally she came to a house where a man came out and

dropped a big Winesap apple into the the bag. The child peered down into the bag and said, "You've done gone and broke ever' damn cookie I had."

*Loyal Jones*

## Demons

The Reverend Donald Welch, former president of Scarritt College for Christian Workers in Nashville, told about lecturing on demons in the seminary. After introducing the subject, he commented that people just don't believe in demons anymore.

"I do," said an old preacher.

"Well, in that case," said Mr. Welch, "how do you

think we ought to deal with the problem of demons?"

"Why," said the reverend gentleman, "convince people that there *are* demons."

Dr. David Nelson
BEREA, KENTUCKY

## Ecumenism

The Baptist pastor called a construction company to come and cut a hole in the outside wall of his office for an air conditioner. He waited, but they did not come. After a while he got a bill for the job. He called up to protest.

The voice on the other end of the phone said, "Just a minute."

After a bit he came back and said, "In the spirit of ecumenism, we cut the hole in the Catholic church."

*Ken McHarg*
LOUISVILLE, KENTUCKY

## In the Minority

A certain fellow had a habit of going to sleep in church, which irritated the preacher. One Sunday, he decided to embarrass him. At the tail end of his sermon, when the offending parishioner was sleeping soundly, he asked everybody who thought they were going to heaven to stand. Everyone stood up except the sleeping man. The preacher smiled slyly and then in a low voice said, "Now, everybody who thinks he's going to hell"— he paused, and then shouted—*"stand up!"*

The sleeping man awoke and jumped to his feet. He looked around and saw that everybody else was seated, looked at the minister and said, "I don't know what we're voting on, Preacher, but it appears that you and me lost."

*Loyal Jones*

## No Fun

*Question:* What is the difference between a Methodist and a Baptist?

*Answer:* There isn't any difference, really. They both sin, but the Methodist can't ever enjoy it.

**Loyal Jones**

*The following five stories are from the recordings of the Reverend George Goldtrap, A* **Funny Thing Happened on the Way to Church** *(Happy Talk Speaking Services, Madison, Tennessee).*

## Precaution

We were fixing to have summer camp in our church, and we were encouraging the kids to fill out cards. We had a questionnaire on the card and had them scattered about the building. At the end of the sermon at the invitation, a lady responded, came up and sat down on the front bench. She picked a card, started filling it out. We have cards for new members there. I went over to talk to her, asked her how we could help her.

She said, "Well, I want to be baptized."

I said, "Well, just put that on the card there."

She said, "I have, but I don't understand this next question."

I looked at the card, and it said, "Can you swim?"

## Passing It On

I was preaching in this church, and this boy would have something negative to say every Sunday, no matter what I preached on. One Sunday he said, "That's about the sorriest sermon I ever heard."

The next Sunday he came by and said, "Do you call that a sermon?"

The third Sunday he said, "That is about the nearest nothing sermon I think I ever heard."

I got so upset that I went to the elders and said, "Gentlemen, every Sunday this man has some negative comment to make about my preaching."

One of them said said, "Oh, don't pay any attention to him. He's just a half-wit. All he can say is what he repeats from other people."

### Recorded Message

We took out the paper towel racks in one church where I preached and put in those electric hand dryers. The very next week somebody put a little note on one of those things, said, "Punch this button for a brief recorded message from our preacher."

### Long Distance?

One Sunday morning, I got up and was looking through the paper, reading the death notices (it always amazes me that people die in alphabetical order), and lo and behold, there was my name. I thought, "I wonder if the elders have seen it."

I got on the phone and called one of them and said, "Have you read the morning paper yet?"

He said, "Yes, sir."

I said, "Did you see my name in the death notices?"

He said, "Yes, I did. Where are you calling from?"

### Married Couples

One time in Bible class I was giving a little quiz, and I said to a fellow, "Can you give me the geographical location of Dan and Beersheba?"

He said, "You mean they are cities?"

I said, "They certainly are."

He said, "Well, I thought they were husband and wife like Sodom and Gomorrah."

## Predestination

A Free-Will Baptist and a Predestinarian Baptist became good friends, and one took the other to a religious conference. As they were going down a long set of stairs, the Predestinarian stumbled and fell and rolled violently down the stairs, hitting with a thud at the bottom.

His friend rushed down, helped him up, and asked, "Are you bad hurt?"

"No," he said, checking himself over, "I think I'm all right."

The Free-Willer said, "But I guess you're glad to get that one behind you, aren't you?"

*Dr. Lee Morris*
BEREA, KENTUCKY

## Mark Twain on Religion

*These comments on religion are taken from Mark Twain Laughing:* **Humorous Anecdotes by and about Samuel L. Clemens,** *ed. P.M. Zall (Knoxville: University of Tennessee Press, 1985). Reprinted by permission of the University of Tennesse Press.*

In church last Sunday I listened to a charity sermon. My first impulse was to give three hundred and fifty dollars: I repented of that and reduced it a hundred; repented of that and reduced it another hundred; repented of that and reduced the remaining fifty to twenty-five; repented of that and dropped to two dollars and a half; when the plate came around at last, I repented once more and contributed ten cents. Well, when I got home, I did wish to goodness I had that ten cents back.

As for me, I hope to be cremated. I made that remark to my pastor once, who said, with what he seemed to think was an impressive manner—
"I wouldn't worry about that if I had your chances."

The village no-'count; very sick. Minister: "You ought to call on God." "Well, I'm so kind of sick & lame I don't git out to call on anybody."

Rev. Alex Campbell, founder of the Campbellites, gently reproved our apprentice, Wales McCormick, on separate occasions, for saying Great God! when Great Scott would have done as well, & for committing the Unforgiven Sin when any other form of expression would have been a million times better. Weeks afterwards, that inveterate light-head had his turn, & corrected the Reverend. In correcting the pamphlet-proof of one of Campbell's great sermons, Wales changed "Great God" to "Great Scott," and changed Father, Son & Holy Ghost to Father, Son and Caesar's Ghost. In overrunning, he reduced it to Father, Son & Co., to keep from overrunning. And Jesus H. Christ.

Adam was but human—this explains it all. He did not want the apple for the apple's sake, he wanted it only because it was forbidden. The mistake was in not forbidding the serpent; then he would have eaten the serpent.

Adam and Eve had many advantages, but the principal one was, that they escaped teething.

What God lacks is convictions—stability of character. He ought to be a Presbyterian or a Catholic or something—not try to be everything.

## Prayer Positions

Three men were talking—three of my neighbors. They were discussing the proper position and attitude for prayer. One said, "You should be on you knees with your head bowed in reverence to the Almighty."

The second man spoke up and said, "Remember that you were created in God's image. The position in which to pray is to stand up looking into the heavens into the face of God and talk to Him as a child to his father."

The third man spoke up and said, "I know nothing about those positions, but the finest praying I ever did was upside down in a well."

*Saunders Guerrant*
**ROANOKE, VIRGINIA**

## Ecumenism

When Huey Long first ran for governor of Louisiana, it was assumed that he, a Baptist from northern Louisiana, would not do well among the Catholics of the southern part of the state, so he was warned to stay away from the subject of religion. But when he spoke down around New Orleans, he got up and told a story about his boyhood:

"I well remember as a boy that every Sunday morning it was my happy task to hitch up the horse to the buggy and take my Catholic grandparents to mass. Then I would bring them home and take my Baptist grandparents to church."

His campaign manager was astonished at this story and remarked, "I didn't know you had Catholic grandparents."

"Don't be silly," said Long, "we didn't even have a horse."

*Dr. William Havard*
BLACKSBURG, VIRGINIA

## Moving Hell

There were two Irishmen come over here. They hadn't ever seen a train. They stopped in a town and put up at a hotel. The hotel sat right by the railroad. Along about midnight a long freight train come roarin' through. Pat jumped up and ran to the window and looked out. The firebox was open and the fire shining and sparks were flying from the engine. This one hadn't more than got by when another came following after it. This one went roaring by when another came along. Pat ran over and shook Mike awake.

"Wake up, Mike," he cried, "they're moving hell. Three loads have already went by."

*Winfred Joseph Kilgore*
BIG LAUREL, VIRGINIA
*Collected by James
Taylor Adams*

*The following two stories are from Allen M. Trout's book,* **Greeting from Old Kentucky: from His Folk-Column in The Courier-Journal,** *Vol. 2 (Frankfort, Kentucky, published by the author, undated).*

## The Witnesses Howled and Hee-Hawed

The Reverend George W. Smith, Pineville, Kentucky, was an old-time Baptist preacher in the counties of Knox and Bell. He was a just man, and his eighty-year life was filled with good works. He was also remembered for his ingenuity. He was always equal to any occasion.

He never liked to lend money to spendthrifts, yet he would not tell a lie. So he named one of his pockets The World. He never carried money in that particular pocket. When he was approached by an unworthy borrower, Brother Smith could reply in good conscience: "I haven't got a cent in The World."

He had a favorite saddle he disliked to lend out. Again, he was equal to the occasion. He owned a farm eight miles away at Flat Lick. He named one end of his barn at home Flat Lick, and in that end of the barn he kept his saddle. Hence, when somebody asked to borrow it, he would reply in truth: "It's at Flat Lick."

But perhaps his greatest feat of ingenuity occurred on Hammons Fork of Stinking Creek in Knox County. Brother Smith was riding his saddle mule, Old Becky, up the fork one day when a girl hailed from her front yard. She and her beau were about ready to be married, the girl said, and she wondered if he could stop and perform the ceremony the next time he came by.

"Have your fellow, your license, and two witnesses here the fourth Sunday in April," Brother Smith said.

The appointed day rolled around. Brother Smith rode up and tied Old Becky at the front gate. The girl met him in tears.

"Oh, Brother Smith," she cried. "Joe is here, and we've got the license. But our witnesses are gone. Uncle Ben broke his leg this morning, and Paw and Maw have gone to see him."

Brother Smith noticed Old Ring, the hound dog, lying on the front porch. He glanced back at his faithful old saddle mule.

"We'll manage all right," he said. "Just join your right hands and repeat after me."

The ceremony over, Brother Smith signed the papers in proper order. And in the space reserved for witnesses, he put down for the benefit of inquiring posterity the names of Becky Smith and Ring Martin.

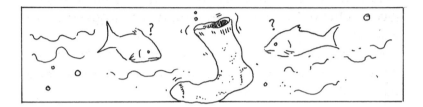

## Polkie Is Unsocked at His Baptism

As the story is told by William Snyder of Anchorage, Kentucky, a Baptist preacher called Brother Joe Harper held a revival in 1892 at Westport, in Oldham County. Polkie Davis got religion and presented himself for baptism in the Ohio River nearby.

Before wading in, Polkie took his shoes off. One of his socks had a big hole in the heel, but the other one was in good shape. Polkie was baptized in due course, and returned to the bank snorting and puffing. But he'd lost one sock in the soft river bottom, the sock without a hole in it. His wife, standing on the bank threw up her hands in dispair and exclaimed: "Lord have mercy, Polkie! You've gone and lost your best sock!"

## Two Little Boys in Church

There were two little boys what lived next door to each other, and they play all the time. They never got some argument about somethin' atall. They never get fist fight on the eye. They love each other. They play all the time, don't go to knuckle junction. That's on Monday, Tuesday, Wednesday, Thursday, Friday, and Saturday, but on

Sunday, whew! Hell broke loose!—because one of them's a Catholic and one's a Methodist, and they got to make a separate from them to brought themselves to church, and they raise so much sand they begin to look like gravel, and that's bad, you know? And their mamas would worry because they goin' to give themselves the fevers. One of the papas, he's smart, you know. School-teacher!

He say, "How come you don't send 'em both to one church one Sunday and both t'other church next Sunday?"

They say, "We never t'ought about that."

The first Sunday, they brought themselves to the Catholic church, and that little Catholic boy, oh, he's proud to have his friend wi' him, I guar-antee. And they walk in to church, and they find a place where they goin' to sit themselves down on a pew. And that little Catholic genuflect, and that's make like you kneel but you don't quite made it.

And that little Methodist boy, never see that before again in his life, he say, "What does that mean, hunh?" That little Catholic boy 'xplain that so carefully, 'cause he want his little friend to enjoy the mass and brought himself back Sunday after next when it is his turn, you know? Then they set themselves down, don't get the seat warm good, then the priest walk in and everybody stood up.

Little Methodist boy never see that again in his life. He say, "What does that mean, hunh?" That little Catholic 'xplain that so carefully, and so sweet the way he do's that, and all through mass, the little Methodist boy want to know what this mean and what that mean and what that mean and what this mean, and that little Catholic, whooh! but he's sweet the way he 'xplain everyt'ing.

The next time they brought themselves to the

Methodist church, an' they walk in there and there's a printed program, and that little Catholic boy never see that before again in his life. He say, "What's that mean, hunh?" An that little Methodist boy, so sweet the way he 'xplain that to his little friend, 'cause he want to be sure he brought himself back wi' him next Sunday when it was his turn.

Then everybody stood up and sing a song, and that little Catholic boy never see that again, he say, "What does that mean, hunh?" That little Methodist boy, so sweet the way that he 'xplain that! And then ever'body set themselves down in the choir right in front of ever-'body to sing a song. That little Catholic boy never see that again before too. He say, "What that mean?" You know, it's always behind in his church. That little Methodist boy 'xplain that real carefully.

The the choir set itself down, and that preaching man walk out in that thing you call a cockpit. He reach there in his pocket, he grab a great big watch and put in front wi' him like that, and that little Catholic boy say, "What's that mean?" That little Methodist boy say, "Not a damn t'ing!"

*Justin Wilson*

From **Cajun Humor**, by Justin Wilson and Howard Jacobs, ©1974. Used by permission of the publisher, Pelican Publishing Company, Inc., Gretna, Louisiana.

## Rewarded Too Late

A man died and went to heaven and St. Peter was showing him around. They passed by this one big room, and inside it there were a bunch of people at banquet tables, feasting on delicious-looking food that was heaped on plates and platters in front of them. "Who are those people?" said the new man. St. Peter said, "Those are the Catholics. They didn't eat a lot on earth, they always had to fast and everything, so they get to make up for it here."

They came to another room and there people were drinking wine, hard liquor, beer; they were reeling from it, and also were dancing wildly the more intoxicated they got. "Who are those people?" "Those are the Baptists. They couldn't drink or dance on earth, so they get to make up for it here."

They came to another room and looked in, and there was the saddest-looking group of people you've ever seen. They were all moping around with long faces. "Who are they?" said the new man. St. Peter said, "Oh, those are the Episcopalians. They've done it all."

*Hope Norman Coulter*
LITTLE ROCK, ARKANSAS

## Check the Hot Place

My grandfather, H.L. Johns, was a Methodist minister, and my mother's name is Helen Hope. My mother says this story isn't true, but according to a family friend, one day when my mother was a little girl she found an umbrella that had been left in the church vestibule. The next Sunday my grandfather announced from the pulpit, "My daughter has found a black umbrella in the vestibule. So if you've lost a black umbrella, you can go to Helen Hope for it."

*Hope Norman Coulter*

## Worse Than He Thought

The little boy noticed a plaque in the back of the church and asked the preacher what it was.

"Oh, those are the church members who died in service," he explained.

"Which," the boy asked, "the ten o'clock or the eleven o'clock one?"

*Dr. Michael Nichols*
LEXINGTON, KENTUCKY

## Unimpressed

The deacon was much impressed with the new minister, and he could hardly wait to tell his neighbor, a skeptical farmer, about him.

"He's got a B.S., an M.S., and a Ph.D.," he said proudly.

"Well, I'm not much on these educated preachers," the farmer said. "We all know what B.S. stands for. M.S. means 'More of the same' and Ph.D. means 'Piled higher and deeper.'"

*Buddy Westbrook*
LONDON, KENTUCKY

## Honest Mistake

The preacher had been invited to dinner at the home of some of his parishioners, and he was seated by the hostess. He had a glass of wine, to which he was unaccustomed. Halfway through the meal he turned to his hostess and said, "I don't want to alarm you, but I think I'm paralyzed. I've been squeezing my leg for about five minutes, and I can't feel a thing."

"Oh, don't worry, that's *my* leg you've been squeezing," she said.

*Loyal Jones*

## Daniel and the Lion's Den

An aunt of mine was teaching Sunday school. She was telling the youngsters about Daniel and the Lion's Den. She had a picture of Daniel standing brave and confident with a group of lions around him. One little eight-year-old girl started to cry.

The teacher said, "Don't cry. The lions are not going to eat Daniel."

The girl said, "That's not what I'm crying about. That little lion over in the corner is not going to get any."

*Saunders Guerrant*
ROANOKE, VIRGINIA

## Coming Attractions

Radio preacher: "Do you want to learn what hell is? Tune in next week. We'll be featuring our organist."

*Dr. Michael Nichols*
LEXINGTON, KENTUCKY

## Improving Agriculture

The district Methodists were holding their annual meeting in a hotel where a group of politicians was having a rally. The cook had fixed pie for the dessert of the Methodists but spiked watermelon for the politicians. The two groups put a strain on the resources of the small-town hotel, and the waitresses got mixed up and took the spiked watermelon to the Methodists. When the cook discovered the mistake, he ordered the waitresses to bring back the watermelon. They came back and told him it was too late, that the preachers were eating the watermelon.

"Well, do they like it?" the cook asked.

"Like it!" one of the waitresses answered. "They're

gobbling it down like it was going out of style, and putting the seeds in their pockets!"

*Loyal Jones*

### Uncertain Pedigree

This unmarried woman had three sets of twins, two, four, and six years old. She got in desperate shape and went to the welfare office to get some help. She filled out the forms and sat down with a social worker for an interview.

"Do you have a husband?" the social worker asked.

"No, ain't never had one."

"Well, who is the father of your children?"

"It depends on which ones you're talking about."

"All right, let's start with the two-year-old twins. Who's their father?"

"Well, I hate to tell you, but it was the preacher down at the valley church."

"What about the four-year-olds?"

"Now, that was the former preacher."

"All right, who is the father of the six-year-olds?"

"Oh my, them two. Ain't they handsome fellows? I just don't know who they belong to. They's born before I got religion."

*Mabel Martin Wyrick*
CORBIN, KENTUCKY

## Cana in Reverse

A moonshiner had hidden his wares out in an outbuilding. One day the revenue officers came and searched until they found the jugs. As they unscrewed the caps to smell the contents, the moonshiner prayed to be delivered from what looked like sure incrimination. After smelling all the jugs, one of the revenuers said, "Why, there's nothing but water in these jugs."

"Hit's a miracle," the moonshiner exclaimed.

*Harry M. Caudill*
WHITESBURG, KENTUCKY

## Hot Pants

My mother used to tell this one about a circuit-rider, and I relate to it because my grandfather was a circuit-rider. They'd go around and preach at different churches, and they'd usually stay at a house next to the church. Sometimes they would leave an extra suit in the house. This circuit-rider had left a suit in the smokehouse. They were having a late fall revival, and he went into the smokehouse to change and then went directly into the church where they had built up a big fire—had the church good and hot. Now, what he didn't know was that there was a wasp's nest in his pants. He started his sermon, began sweating and then squirming. All of a sudden he ran down the aisle and screamed, "I've got love in my heart but hell in my britches!"

*Billy Wilson*
BEREA, KENTUCKY

## Besetting Sins

Three preachers went fishing. They were out in a boat most of the day and got to be good friends. Soon they

67

began confiding personal matters and problems they had in their congregations. After a while, one of them said, "We all have our weaknesses. Let's tell ours. I confess that I like a little nip now and then."

The second one said, "I like to look at the women."

They turned expectantly to the third, who said, "I like to tell tales, and I can't wait to get to get to shore."

*Billy Wilson*

## A Bargain

A man and his son went to church, and when they came out the man was complaining that the service was too long, the preacher no good, and the singing off-key. Finally the little boy said, "Daddy, I thought it was pretty good for a dime."

*Billy Wilson*

## Commandments

The preacher was teaching the men's Sunday school class on the subject of the Ten Commandments. When he discussed "Thou Shalt Not Steal," a man on the front row became distracted and agitated, but when he got to "Thou Shalt Not Commit Adultery," he relaxed and started paying attention again. The preacher saw the man after class and asked if anything was wrong.

"Oh, no, Preacher, it's all right. When you mentioned the one about stealing, I got upset because I thought somebody had taken my umbrella, but when you got to the other one about adultery, I remembered where I left it."

*Loyal Jones*

## Going Prepared

A man was going down the road one day when he met an old friend, all dressed up from head to toe, and he had a Bible under his arm.

"Where are you going?"

"Going to Atlanta. I been hearing about the sporting houses down there, with all them good-looking women, and I aim to go have me a time."

"Well, if you're going to the sporting houses, how come you're carrying a Bible?"

"If them sporting houses are as interesting as I hear tell, I may just stay over till Sunday."

**Dr. William Deal**
HUNTINGTON, WEST VIR-
GINIA

## Preacher Talk

An old Baptist preacher was crossing the street when a hot-rodding teenager roared down the street, grazed the old preacher, and caused him to fall into the gutter.

The preacher jumped up, shook his fist, and shouted, "You son of a bitch—have you no respect for a preacher?"

*Loyal Jones*

## A Question of Virgin Birth

A young pastor took a rural church. Being recently out of the seminary with its heady theological discussions, he set up a series of lectures to deliver to his flock on Thursdays evenings. His first topic was "Immaculate Conception," and he gave what he imagined to be an inspired and thorough lecture on the subject. When he had finished, he asked if there were any questions, not

69

really expecting any. A woman in the back raised her hand and inquired timidly, "Uh, what are its advantages?"

*Loyal Jones*

## Faint Praise

The minister had preached a vigorous and thoughtful sermon, and several of the congregation rushed up to congratulate him. One lady gushed, "Preacher, every sermon you preach is better than the next one!"

*Dr. Troy Eslinger*
JACKSON, KENTUCKY

## Loved Peanuts

The new young pastor was calling on the elderly who could no longer go to church. His first call was to Aunt Sally, who was quite old and in a nursing home. He was somewhat nervous, and he kept eating peanuts from a bowl beside her bed. When he got up to leave, he noticed that he had eaten all of the peanuts.

"I'm so sorry. I ate up all of your peanuts," he stammered.

"Oh, that's all right," Aunt Sally said. "I'd already gummed all of the chocolate off of them anyhow."

*Shirley Jones*
MARBLE, NORTH CARO-
LINA

## The Masquerade

We wanted to have a masquerade party. We said other people are having them, they sound like fun and we'd never had one.

So we met in a fellow's house; he lived way out a country road. We were goin' to meet out there and have that party. Well, I dressed up like the devil, put on a little red devil outfit, little horns and everything, and I was goin' out the road at night, and a storm came up, and I needed a place to get in out of the weather. I darted in a little building there beside the road, and it just so happened, it was a little country church, and they were right in the midst of a big revival meetin'. Law! You can imagine what a commotion it caused when I jumped up in the door with my devil outfit on. They went out doors, windows, anyplace they could get out. One fellow right up toward the front jumped up, got his coattail hung on the seat, and couldn't get away. He threw up both arms and said, "I've been a member of this church for twenty-five years, but I've been on your side all along!"

*Dr. Carl Hurley*
LEXINGTON, KENTUCKY

*From his recording **Looking for the Humor**
(Louisville: McKinney Associates, 1987)*

## The Old Reprobate

An old reprobate down in Tennessee died. He hadn't been good to his wife, had neglected his children, had never darkened the door of a church, and was hardly sober a day of his life. When he died, they had a graveside service. In this particular town, they had a sage who was always called upon to say a few words when someone died whom he had known all of his life. People wondered what the sage would say about the old reprobate when they didn't see anything good about him. But the sage got up and said, "Well now, beloved, you know he wasn't as bad *all* the time as he was *most* of the time!"

*Dr. Lee Morris*
BEREA, KENTUCKY

## Charitable Contribution

An agent of the Internal Revenue Service called a preacher and said, "One of your church members, Sam Harris, put down on his tax return that he had made a contribution of fifteen hundred dollars to your church. Is that true?"

The preacher thought a minute and then replied, "If he didn't, he will."

*Loyal Jones*

## Noah's Wife

A preacher, ending his sermon, announced that he would preach on Noah and his Ark on the following Sunday and gave the scriptural reference for the congregation to read ahead of time. A couple of mean boys noticed something interesting about the placement of the story of the Flood in the Bible. They slipped into the church and glued two pages of the pulpit Bible together. On the next Sunday, the preacher got up to read his text.

"Noah took unto himself a wife," he began, "and she was"—he turned the page to continue—"three hundred cubits long, fifty wide and thirty high." He paused, scratched his head, turned the page back and read it silently, turned the page. Then he looked up at his congregation and said,

"I've been reading this old Bible for nigh on to fifty years, but there are some things in it that are hard to believe."

*Loyal Jones*

## *Strategic Planning*

President William G. Frost of Berea College remembered one Jackson County, Kentucky, preacher around the turn of the century who laid down some of the wisdom which should be a guide in planning a "protracted" meeting. "Don't give any notice beforehand and don't keep preaching more than five days." Why? "Because, stranger, there are a heap of no-count fellers always hangs around a church meeting like flies round a sorghum keg, and a little moonshine whiskey will play the devil amongst them. Now if they know there is going to be a meeting, they will pack their stills in some nearby hollow and have the critter ready. But we begin the meeting without warning and hold just five days, and it takes five days for them to make a run of moonshine."

*Jess D. Wilson*
POSSUM TROT, KENTUCKY

# Sermon Parodies

## Where the Lions Roareth and the Whangdoodle Mourneth

*This piece was performed by Bascom Lamar Lunsford of Leicester, North Carolina, and is attributed to William P. Brannan, an artist and newspaper writer. A version appears in* **The Harp of a Thousand Strings; or, Laughter for a Lifetime,** *ed. S.P. Avery (New York: Dick & Fitzgerald, Publishers, 1858), pp. 224-26.*

*This type of sermon existed about the time flatboats used to run up and down the Mississippi, say in 1850. I'm giving it here because as it sounds—I'm not referring to the meaning—it is similar to a type of sermon which sometimes may be heard in certain communities in the great Southern Appalachian country. Imagine a country audience with the minister ready to start his sermon...*

Bretheren and sisteren, I do not come before you this evening to engage in any grammar talk or college high-falutin', but I come to prepare a pervarse generation for the day of wrath, and my text, when you find it, you'll find it 'twixt the lids of this old Bible, from the first chapter of Second Chronicles to the last chapter of Timothy-Titus, and when you find it, you'll find it in these words, "And they shall gnaw a file and flee into the mountains of Hespudam, where the lions roareth and the whangdoodle mourneth for its first-born."

Now, my bretheren and sisteren, there's different kinds of files. There's the rat-tailed file, and there's the handsaw file, and there's the crosscut file, and there's the profile and the defile [*here the good preacher starts chanting*], but the text says, "They shall gnaw a file and flee into the mountains of Hespudam, uh, where the lions roareth and the whangdoodle mourneth for its first-born, uh."

And bretheren and sisteren, there are many kinds of dams. There's Amsterdam, and then there's Rotterdam, and there's Beaverdam, but the last of all and the worst of all, uh, my bretheren, is "I don't give a damn," but the text says that "They shall gnaw a file and flee into the mountains of Hespudam, uh, where the lions roareth and the whangdoodle mourneth for its first-born, uh."

Now, my bretheren and sisteren, this reminds me of the man who lived upon the north fork of Little Pine Creek in Madison County, North Carolina. He had a little mill, but he ground a heap of corn, but one night the fountain of the great deep was broken up, and the windows of heaven were opened and the rains descended, the winds came and washed that little man's mill to Kingdom Come. He got up the next morning and told the good old wife of his bosom that he wasn't worth a damn! But the text says that "they shall gnaw a file and flee into the mountains of Hespudam uh, where the lions roareth and the whangdoodle mourneth for its first-born uh."

My bretheren and sisteren, this doesn't mean the howling wilderness where John the Hardshelled Baptist fed on locusts and wild asses, but it means the city of New Orleans, the mother of harlots and hard-lots, where corn is six bits a bushel one day and nary a red the next, and where thieves and pickpockets go skitting about like weasels in a barnyard, and where honest men are sca'cer'n hens' teeth, and where a woman once took up your beloved preacher and bamboozled him out of a hundred and twenty-seven plunks in three jerks of the eye and the twinkling of a sheep's tail, but she can't do it again, hallelujah!

## A Doctrine Is a Doctrine

The old Hardshelled preacher loved to preach about baptism, and he waxed long and frequently on the principle of total immersion. He scoffed at the Methodists and others who thought otherwise. The congregation got kind of tired of these sermons, and the head deacon thought he had a plan to steer him in another direction. He approached him and reminded him that many of the old-time preachers relied entirely on the inspiration of God in selecting the text for their sermons and would open the Bible at random and then preach on the verse that first appeared to them. The old preacher said he believed that too and would use that method the following Sunday.

When it came time for him to preach, he strode to the pulpit, stuck his finger into the Bible, opened it, and read, "And the voice of the turtle was heard in the land." Without a pause he leapt into his sermon:

"Oh bretheren and sisteren, this mornin' as I was a-

heading to church, I had to cross the bridge over the creek back yonder. The sun was shinin' down on the rocks there, and the mud turtles was a-sunning their-selves on them rocks. I stopped for a minute on yon side to watch them, but when I started acrost that there bridge, them turtles went into that water *kerplunk!* Now bretheren and sisteren, they didn't reach down there and get a little water and sprinkle on their heads. No, and they didn't just go halfway into the water. No, when they went in they went all the way in. And there, bretheren and sisteren, you have your doctrine of total immersion!"

*Loyal Jones*

## The Collectin' Parson

King Owen, who worked with me in a tent show more than fifty years ago, had a semblance of it, and I fooled with it, and like Topsy, it grew. I've never seen it written or performed anywhere else.

> *Now, we got a preacher down at our church,*
> *And he shore can preach out loud.*
> *And pray—why, that man can pray till every head is*
>     *bowed.*
> *He visits the sick, makes them all feel grand.*
> *He's one fine preacher, he's one fine man,*
> *Calls on the neighbors and cheers every soul.*
> *But when collectin' time comes on Sunday,*
> *Huh uh, that's when he goes for the goal.*
> *Now, one Sunday morning to church we went,*
> *And each woman took along her man,*
> *And our parson preached in a voice so loud*
> *As only a preacher can.*
> *Come time to take up the collection,*
> *He called on Sister Jones. "Miz Jones,*

Get up now and we'll shake down these lazy bones."
So the ladies then they started to pass the plates to all.
Our parson jumped up and said, "Whoa,
I got somethin' to tell y'all.
Now, there's a certain man settin' down here in his pew,
And he's doin' wrong each day.
He drinks bad gin, takes the ladies 'round.
In his pleasures he's just too gay.
Now, if that man don't drop a silver dollar in the pan,
I'm goin' to get right up in the pulpit and name that
   man."
So the ladies they started in to pass the plates again,
And the way the dollars hit that pan, you'd think it was
   rain.
When counted up it was ninety-six dollars shinin' up in
   sin.
Our parson said, "Thanks y'all, now let the prayin'
   begin."
But I never dropped no dollar in that pan,
'Cause I never had that kind of dough,
But I wrote a little note and snuck it in,
Sayin', "Parson, I'll see you in a day or so."

**Bradley Kincaid**
POINT LEAVELL, KEN-
TUCKY,
AND SPRINGFIELD, OHIO

## *Elder Eatmore's Sermon on Throwing Stones*

*This parody is based on a recording by Charles E. Mack on Columbia 50061-D, 1928. Courtesy of Robert Cogswell, Nashville, Tennessee.*

*Elder:* I take my text this morning from the Eleventh of the Ecclesiastices, "Let ye who is mostly without sin, throw the first rock." Course what it really says is let him

*80*

cast the first stone. Now, I ain't taking no chances on y'all misunderstanding me. For twenty years you been throwing rocks at one another. But you wasn't satisfied. No, you had to commence throwing them at me, and I ain't a-going to warn you no more. In the language of that great prophet, Henry Ford, "Watch your bolts, watch your bolts."

What did Nicodemus say? I say, what did Nicodemus say? He say, "Wash me and I shall be whiter than snow." They's a lot of you here this morning that thinks you been washed, but you ain't even been sponged. On one night last week, I think it was about midnight, a certain brother—he's sitting right here—was a-coming down the road a-toting a bag, and he see another brother coming over the fence a-toting a bag. Now neither one of these brothers spoke, but the sound in the bag of the brother on the fence indicated that he had secured for himself the main obstacle for a Thanksgiving dinner. Un hah! Now, that other certain brother had in his bag a member of the same family, but it was not generally the kind of bird used for a Thanksgiving dinner, and this filled that certain brother's heart so full of jealousy and malice that he goes straight home and tells his wife what he sees, and that does it. His wife tells her sister, and her sister tells her friend, and the first thing I know, ever' member of this congregation is whispering around here that I! me! stole a turkey. Huh, huh, huh, preposterous!

In the future, any of y'all throws rocks at me, I'm going

to throw them right back at you, and when I starts to throw 'em, friends, I shall miss nobody. Ah, there's silence. Now that certain brother I been talking 'bout, will kindly lead us in prayer.

*Brother:* Sure now, the Scriptures says that who that God would at last destroy, he would first make mad, and Elder Eatmore sure is acting crazy. On last Thursday night, who did I almost have to tote home? I almost had to carry home bodily? And Lord, he was so full of apple-jack. Who was it, O Lord, I say, who was it who stole Elijah's money? I say who was it, Lord, who stole Elijah's money and lost it playin' five-up? Who was it—?

*Elder:* Doxology! Use all the doors! Use all the doors! We are all leavin' now. We are all leavin' now.

## The Substitute Parson

*The next parody is from a recording by Chic Sale on Victor 22103-A, 1927. Courtesy of Robert Cogswell, Nashville, Tennessee.*

I'm glad to see so many here this beautiful Sunday morning, but I am very sorry to announce that our minister is ill. However, I have volunteered to take his place. I will do the best that I can. I am not a minister, as you all know. I am an undertaker.

I will open with the regular, customary announcements. The regular Monday night choir practice of this church will be held on Tuesday night, instead of Friday. All members of the choir please note. Mrs. George M. Snark of this church wishes to thank all her friends who so kindly assisted in the death of her husband. A beautiful thought!

Brother Frank W. Quick, who was thrown out of our church on account of dancing, is back with us again in good standing. Dancing is against the rules of our church. The brother was caught hop-scotching around. . . . He was immediately waited on by our committee, and his alibi was so good we have taken the brother back into the fold, and I congratulate the brother. His alibi was that he did not know what he was doing at the time. That finishes the announcements.

I'm taking for my topic this morning "Ambition Without Cause." I have selected, and will read from, the Mother Goose book of our childhood days—"Old Mother Hubbard":

Old Mother Hubbard, she went to the cupboard
To get her to get her poor dog a bone,
When she got there, the cupboard was bare,
And the poor little dog had none.

The text is, "Ambition Without Cause, Old Mother Hubbard." Mother Hubbard, you see, was old. There being no mention of Mr. Hubbard, we are to presume that she is alone, a widow—a poor, friendless, helpless widow. Yet, did she despair? No, dear friends, I am happy to say no, that she went to the cupboard—-Oh, isn't this beautiful? We have seen that she was old and lonely, and now we further see that she was poor. Oh, mark these words—ah-h-h. The cupboard—not one of the cupboards, not the right-hand cupboard, nor the left-hand cupboard, nor the one above, nor the one below—but just the one, the one solitary, measly little cupboard that the poor widow had!

Now, the question arises . . ., the question, why? Why, did she go to the cupboard? There's the catch! There's the sticker! There's where our brightest minds have fallen down, but go a step further. I will go so far now as to picture . . . to imagine that we are dogs, the poor dog lounging there in the corner. . . . He's looking wistfully at the cupboard, and the poor widow is going forward with hope, with expectations, maybe. Dear friends, she was old, but she was ambitious and full of pep!

That finishes my talk. While we now rise . . ., brother, would you pass the plate, we'll sing that well-known hymn, "Go Tell Aunt Rhody."

## The Preachments

Dr. Lee Morris, who contributes the following, is campus minister at Berea College, Berea, Kentucky.

I was privileged to be raised on a farm in Tennessee. I was also privileged as a "young'un" to attend several small country churches. Many times the sermons were long and wandering. The preachers, usually self-taught and the more knowledgeable ones among us, believed the Bible from cover to cover—and many of them preached it that way—from cover to cover—in each sermon! If I dozed off when the preacher was around Exodus, and then woke up and found him around Malachi or Matthew, I might as well go back to sleep—I was going to be there for some while longer before he reached Revelation! As I grew older, I of course learned to appreciate the preachers, the Bible, the church folk; the taproot of my faith is deepest in those rural church experiences. When I went away to college to "make a preacher" of myself, I was also heir to a sense of humor from my farm family and those country church folk who knew better than to take themselves or anything else this side of heaven too seriously. I put together the following humorous "preachments" to celebrate my roots, to entertain like-minded friends, to help the many other folk with similar backgrounds to remember and rejoice, and just to enjoy "my own fool self."

Brethren and sistern, before I get into the preachments this morning, I need to make two announcements. Now, to be fair to all concerned, I will make the second announcement first—and the first announcement second, but real slow. Thus it is that the first shall be last and the last first. Now the first announcement concerns the deacons of the church, both of y'all.—Will you deacons please recollect to meet with the pastor, who is still me, after the service this morning to discuss what can be did about our coal supply for the oncoming winter. As y'all know, last year we went out yander 'crosst the pasture to the railroad tracks and picked up the coal off the railroad tracks—but this year the Methodists have gone on before us and the tracks are barren! So recollect this coal meeting with the pastor after the service this morning.

Now, the second renouncement—uh, a-nouncement—concerns the good ladies of the church in the mission soci-ty. Will y'all please recollect to meet with Sister Pastor's Wife—after dinner, 'round two-thirty, on my back porch—to discuss what can be did about this epidemic of gossip spreading like a dust storm through our good community. So don't you ladies forget your gossip meeting this evening!

Now, before I get into the preachments this morning, I

also need to make a explanation about how I'm gonna deliver myself of the preachments. I'm gonna be preaching from inspired recomemberandum this morning, rather than from my usual notes, because I got my glasses broke in about the second round of a scheduled ten-rounder with my wife in the kitchen last night, and I can't see nothing much atall. Hmmm—come to think on it, this may be what that gossip meeting's all about this evening!

Now, I want to take you with me to the Book of Lukie—spelled L-U-K-E—Lukie. That's like in the saying, "Well, lookie heah—well, lookie yander." Now, in the Book of Lukie we find a family—but it don't give the name of the family—however therefore, we all know the name of the youngest son in the family, what was Proggigal, the proggigal son—P-R-O-double G-I-G-A-L: Proggigal.

Now, like most of us folks, Proggigal was a hard-working farm boy, but he didn't take no pleasure in being heavy-laden or sore perplexed. One day he was plowing in the field and he said, to hisself, "Self?" And his self saith unto him, "Speak, for thy servant heareth!" And Proggigal said to hisself, "What must I do to be delivered from my sore oppression?" And his self saith unto Proggigal, "You know a laborer is worthy of his hire—that is the law of the land, the tradition of the elders, the way of all saints—and, besides, it makes good sense." So Proggigal said, "Well, what do you want me to do about it?" And his self saith to him, "Go to your father and require at his hand your portion that rightly belongs to you and to no other and let him see your face hereabouts no more henceforth!" And Proggigal said, "Well, I'll try to keep all that in mind." So Proggigal went to his dear old father and said, "Daddy! Gimme that portion what by rights belongs to me and to no other

and you'll see my face hereabouts no more henceforth—
selah." He threw the "selah" in there to make himself
sound a little religious—which he wasn't a mile close to
being.

Now, Proggigal's father was a goodly man who stood a
head and shoulders above all in his community, his
heart was set on no sort of evil, his doctrine was sound,
and in him there was no bile. So almost nobody liked
him. Least of all his son, Proggigal. When Proggigal's
father heard the words of his son, his countenance fell.
But in a minute he picked up his countenance, and he
said to his son, "This is a hard saying and I must fast and
pray upon it." So he went into the wilderness to fast and
pray, and he fasted for forty days and for forty nights.
Now, you might wonder why he fasted for so long a
time—forty days and forty nights. It was because he was
a slow faster. But eventual, he come forth from the wilderness and called unto his son, "C'mere, boy!" So he
did. And Proggigal's father said, "Son, you have rightly
said, a laborer is worthy of his hire—that is the law of the
land, the tradition of the elders, the way of the saints,
and besides, it makes good sense—but I still don't like it
all that much. But whatsoever you ask of me, that will I
do. Take this portion that rightly belongs to you and to
no other and let me see your face hereabouts no more
henceforth—go your way, but we will look for a second
coming that no man knows the time thereof as yet." So
with these words his father bestowed his blessing upon
Proggigal and after his father had blessed him out, Proggigal took his leave—and everything else not nailed
down—and set his face straightway toward a far country.
Now, he had journeyed about a sabbath day's journey,
because it was of a Saturday—when he drew nigh unto a
grea-a-at body of water that no man could number. So
greaaat was this body of water that he couldn't go 'round

to the right, and he couldn't go 'round to the left, and he couldn't go over because they hadn't inventioned airplanes yet, and he couldn't go under because they hadn't inventioned submarines yet, and he couldn't swim, and he warn't even thirsty. But was Proggigal discouraged and desirous of heart to turn back after having put his hand to the plow? Of course not. And "Why?" you might ask. Why? Because he had faith— faith that could remove mountains—and if it could work on the mountains, it could work on the waters! So Proggigal stepped forth in faith and put his feet into the waters—and the waters straightway separated one side from t'other—no doubt also from the stench thereof—as it was of a Saturday and he hadn't yet had his Sat'dy bath.

Now, Proggigal pressed on in his journey until he come to the big city what was named Babylon. Now in the big city of Babylon, like in most of our modernized big cities today, there was many pretty girls for Proggigal out wherewithal to go. And he had come a'purpose— and looked upon the field as white unto harvest. But there was one pretty girl above all the rest that he loved the most—she turned his head so quick it jerked a crick in his neck. Her name was Delilah.

Now, Delilah was a sleek, sassy, seductive, solicitous, secularist Philistine. Delilah didn't have no tradition atall of "Thou shalt not." Her tradition was "Thou shalt—if thou canst." And she couldst—and she didst. She believed what is to be will be—if'n you'll help it a little. And she believed in doing her part. She believed you should put your practice into belief. And she didn't need all that much practice, neither.

Now, one night Delilah and Proggigal went walking arm in arm together under the full moon in the Garden of Eden—and the sun stood still—to give them more time! And Delilah said to Proggigal, "Proggigal." And Proggigal said, "Here am I, sinned me!" And Delilah said, "Well, Belshazzar the king—is giving a little shindig at his palace of a Friday night—and I got me two little ol' tickets to go—would you like to go with little ol' me to Belshazzar's shindig?" Now Proggigal of course had come a'purpose, and he was natural given to shindigs. So he said to Delilah, "Whithersoever thou goest, there I will go."

So they did. They went to Belshazzar's shindig of a Friday night. Proggigal wore one of them native togas, which was something like a split sheet hanging down to his knees—which was more than you could say for Delilah—she wore her gownless evening strap. And before they hardly knowed who was whose and what was where, everybody at the shindig was carrying on something fierce in a wild drunken spree. It looked like they didn't care anything a'tall about making fools of theirselfs. Then all of a suddenly, a hand started writing on the wall—and the writing come to this: "Menny, menny—tickle your parson!" Now the people were throwed into great frightments and there was much wailing and snatching of teeth.

Now, Proggigal was a pleasure-pursuing man till he was scared, then he experienced a strange and sudden—and temporary—transformation into a praying man. But he warn't never no good to pray in public—so he passed through their mist somehow—you see, there's rain and there's fog and there's mist—so he passed through their mist—and he run on out to the hillside there to pray by hisself.

Out on the hillside before Proggigal could bend a word or say a knee—down the hillside come this stampeding herd of hogs perplexed with devils. Now, so great was this herd of hogs that Proggigal couldn't go 'round to the right, and he couldn't go 'round to the left, and he couldn't go over, and he shore 'nough didn't want to go under. And he wasn't partial to deviled ham. But was Proggigal discouraged? Was he desirous of heart to turn back after having come so far? You bet your tithe he was! Because by this time he had committed the unpossible sin, which for there is no forgiveness. So he had to meet the devil and take his comeuppance. . . and the deviled hogs come a-rolling over him and a-rolling over him—until they dumped him into the hog pen at the foot of the mountain.

Now, Proggigal was knocked unconscious from his fall—but you know what it says in the Book of Lukie: "he come to hisself." He was knocked out but he come to there by hisself in the hogpen. Proggigal saw what kind of a postion he was in—so he got out of that position into a more comfortable position. And he cried, "Oh, woe is me! woe is me!" And "is me" wasn't his horse he was trying to stop, neither. It was his condition. "Oh, woe is me! Woe is me!" he cried. "Here I am with one foot in the grave and the other one on a slick shuck!" He then said to hisself, "Self? Self, are you still with me?" His self saith unto him, "I will be with you unto the end." Proggigal said, "Well, I think we're almost there. I'm even having bad luck with praying, anymore." So he said to hisself, "I need a sign whether or not I can go back home." His self saith unto him, "This will be a sign unto you—put a fleece on the post over there and if it rains tonight and the fleece is dry in the morning, that means you can go home." Proggigal said to hisself, "That ain't much of a sign." His self saith unto him, "You ain't much of a sight right now yourself." So Proggigal took what was given and went out and killed a fleece—and put its hide on the post. That night the winds blew and the rains fell. The next morning Proggigal went out to see if his fleece was dry—and the wind had blowed it away. But he took that for a sign anyway—to be up and away. So he arose from where he was, which is the only place a man can arise from—and started on his journey home.

Now, as he journeyed, it began to rain—and it rained for forty days and for forty nights. Now again we hear of forty days and forty nights, like when Proggigal's father prayed and fasted in the wilderness. There's a lesson in that—the father has eaten sour grapes and the son's edge is set on teeth. Proggigal floated around in a basket of reeds on top of the water—for a month or a month and a half or two months—it's hard to tell exactly how long without my glasses. But eventual, he landed on Mount Ararat with a olive branch in his mouth. After he lit on Mount Olive with a rat in his mouth—the waters went down, and so did Proggigal—into the wilderness.

Now, y'all know how it is in the wilderness. You can't see where you're going and you can't go where you're seeing, so you're apts to get lost. And he did—and he wandered for forty years in the wilderness. (And I don't know what that "forty" may mean—except that it may seem to you like I've been wandering around myself here for forty minutes.) But Proggigal wandered around in the wilderness for forty years, running from the mad Egyptians who thought he'd stolen their golden calf. After he wandered for forty years in the wilderness, Proggigal was took up in a whirlwind that blowed him acrosst the Jordan River and onto a high mountain where his hair caught in some tree limbs—which brought him to somewhat of a sudden hair-raising stop. Then Amos, a pincher of sycamore trees, come along and pinched the sycamore tree and made it wither, so that Progiggal's hair come loose from the withered limbs. From the high mountain he could see from whence he had come and whereunto he needed to go— but he was too tired to tote hisself any further, so he took a rock for his pillow and laid down and fell into a deep slumber and had a dream. And in his dream he saw a ladder stretched from earth to heaven—and on top of the ladder was his dear old father, saying, "Son, the spirit and the bride say, 'Come.' The spirit and the bride say, 'Come.'" Proggigal woke up from his slumber and said, "Why, Daddy, if I'd knowed you got married again, I'd-a tried to be home for the shindig!" Proggigal still hadn't lost his yen for shindigs and suchlike. So he arose from where he was, which is still the only place a man can arise from—and proceeded on his journey home.

Well, eventual, Proggigal reached home again. And so great was the merriment of the father to see him that he called out, "Oh, absent son, my absent son—who was gone ain't gone no more, who was dead ain't dead no more—he just smells that way." To celebrate his son's return home, the father killed their fatted calf and throwed a big bar-be-que and invited all the neighbors to come to the feast. But y'all know how neighbors do— they make excuses. One neighbor said, "Have me excused, I can't come because I have bought oxen, and I have to go get them out of the ditch." A second neighbor said, "I have bought land and must go see it; and lo, the summer is ended and the harvest is past, and I haven't even made the down payment yet." A third neighbor had just got married and he said he warn't particular hungry. Finally, they went out into the highways and hedges and invited all the preachers to come to eat—and great was the multitude thereof.

Now, it would be fitting for me to end the preachments on this note of great joy, but there is a deep question in y'all's minds that you want me to answer—and I am a preacher that don't let no question pass through our minds unanswered, lest we become too proud of our humility. And that question is: What happened to Delilah? Hmmm-huh! I will set my mind now to tell you what happened to Delilah. When the judgment of the Lord fell on Belshazzar's palace that Friday night, Delilah's servants, the eunuchs—who warn't too busy at the party because they always keep watch over their own by night—helped her escape by lifting her out through a window in a basket.—Then she too passed wherewithal through the mist and repaired herself to her upper room. There she was getting ready to go to bed when all of a suddenly down the Milky Way come Gabriel the angel riding in a fiery chariot with a big wheel turning in a little wheel—and he skidded to a stop just below Delilah's window. Gabriel got out of his chariot and she run to the window to see what was the ruckus. Gabriel looked up and called out, "Who is that up there?" She said, "It is Delilah." Gabriel said, "That's who I thought it was, because like unto you there is no other and your reputation is spread abroad in the land. And I have come to take a religious census. Who is on the Lord's side?" And Delilah's eunuchs yelled out, "Well, Delilah sure ain't—don't sign her up for nothing. She don't go to Sunday school or church and she ain't gonna pledge to tithe, neither!" So Gabriel told the eunuchs, "Throw her down!" So they throwed her down. Gabriel said, "Throw her down again!" So they throwed her down again—and all sum total they throwed her down seventy times seven—and the remains were twelve basketsfull—

and the question that remains today that no one can answer is: Now, whose wife is she gonna be in the Judgment?!

Selah! And may all your preachments be a joy to hear.

## Little David

*The "Little David" sermon was given to me many years ago by a minister who said that he could authenticate it. The story is about a rounder in the community who is converted in a revival meeting and decides to start preaching. This is how his first sermon goes.*

Little David's pappy said to him one day, "We ain't heard from the boys for quite a spell. Why don't ye run there to the army camp and see how they're a-doing?"

"All right, Pappy," said Little David, and off he took hisself down the road to see his brothers.

He got down there, and they's all a-standing around with their hands in their pockets, weren't doing a thing. Little David walked up to King Saul and said, "King Saul, why ain't you all fighting?"

"Ah," he said, "them Philadelphians over there have got a great old big giant named Goly-ath. He's been roaring and a-bellering around here and wanting to fight one of our men, and he says if he whips our man, they win the battle, and if our man wins, we win the battle."

"Well gosh-a-mighty, why ain't you a-fighting?"

"Ah," he said, "all of my men are yaller. They ain't a-wanting to fight."

"Why," David said, "you give me leave and I'll fight your old Golyath."

"Get out of here, you little shrimp. You're too little."

"Never might that shrimp stuff. Just give me leave, and I'll fight old Golyath."

Now old King Saul knowed there wasn't no use in arguing with that old boy when he got his back up. He says, "All right." They brung him out an armor, and he said, "Get that tin suit out of here." They brung him out a sword. "Naw," he said, "I ain't a-wanting your swords neither." He just walked off down the holler a piece, and purty soon here come that old giant a-roaring and a-bellering, "Oh, Little David, I got you now, boy!"

Man, if that'd a been me, there'd a been a blue streak there yet, and a little yaller'n too, 'cause I'd a lit a shuck out of there. But Little David was just as cool as a cucumber. He just retched down there in that holler and picked up about five little old stones, and he put one in that slingshot of his'n, and he drawed back and hit that son of a bitch right between the eyes and killed him deader'n hell! Walked over there and grabbed that old giant's sword and chopped his block off, and here he come with it, just as proud as a peacock, walked up to old King Saul, and he said, "Here, Saul, here's you old Goly-ath!"

*Edward Thomas*
KEYSTONE, WEST VIR-
GINIA, AND
DELANO, CALIFORNIA

# Devil Tales

The Devil is prominent in folktales, in which Jack or other folk heroes deal successfully with him, and he is also the subject of sermons in rural churches, even if he isn't mentioned much in the mainline ones anymore. Here are a few folktales dealing with Old Scratch from both black and white traditions.

## The Devil

*This tale was collected by Rose Thompson in about 1945 from Uncle Wright Boyer, of Hancock County, Georgia, and is from* **Hush Child! Can't You Hear the Music?** *by Rose Thompson (Athens: University of Georgia Press, 1982, pp. 2–5). Reprinted by permission of the University of Georgia Press.*

The Devil was plenty smart back in the old days, and bless your time, he was one of the greatest songsters in heaven. Surely was. He used to lead the singing choir up there in heaven and sometimes he would hop up on a pole and whistle just like a mockingbird. There just wasn't any stopping him. He used to issue out the blessing three times a day amongst the angels up there, and he named himself Champion Luther. If ever there was a sight, he was one.

Then he got to cutting up powerful bad; said if he didn't take that kingdom, he was going to build a kingdom to the north side of that one about a span above the stars. And that proves it was a starry heaven. Um-m-m-hum!

Well, then, after he had done all that talking, he up and banished himself. After a while Michael was standing by the Royal where God was seated and he looked out and saw the Devil coming back and he said, "Behold! The great dragon is coming to take vengeance on our kingdom, all stained in hallowed blood."

And when he got there the Devil raised a war. He fought and cut up scandalous and backed the angels up under the throne. God was sitting there watching from the Royal.

And then the Devil disappeared again. And when he had come back Michael looked out and saw him again. And he said, *"Be-ho-o-old!* The great dragon is coming again!"

God didn't say anything to Michael the other time, but this time He said, "Michael, you go out and meet him and put him out of here. If you have to reach back there in my wardrobe and take seven bolts of thunder and put against him. Put him out of here, Michael! Put him out!"

God was just sitting on the Royal watching to see what was going to happen. Michael grabbed the Devil and the Lord told him to put him out. Michael threw the Devil over the bannister of time. Then he tipped over and peeped way down and saw the Devil where he had dropped to and he said, "Lord, the great dragon fell way down to torment."

The the Lord said, "Michael, hurry right on down and beat the Devil to earth, and chain him tight and fast." And that is what Michael did and the Devil has been chained ever since.

You say you believe it—you might as well too, for it is written in the Bible for you to read.

## Willie and the Devil

*The following tale was collected by James Taylor Adams from John Martin Kilgore of Wise, Virginia, on January 20, 1942. He had heard it from his father sixty years before. From the James Taylor Adams papers, John Cook Wyllie Library, Clinch Valley College, Wise Virginia. Courtesy of Robin Benke. This tale and many others appear in* **Outwitting the Devil: Jack Tales from Wise County, Virginia,** *ed. Charles L. Perdue, Jr. (Santa Fe: Ancient City Press, 1987).*

One time there was a young feller named Willie. He was a pretty rowdy sort of boy and he got to gambling. Got so that he'd banter everybody he met for a game of cards. Preachers or just anybody.

One day he was going along when he met up with the Devil. So he tackled him for a game of cards. They sot down and went to playing. The Devil beat Willie seven straight games. Willie then turned it on him and beat him seven. The Devil didn't like it, so he told Willie that he'd have to be at his house by the next Saturday night sure or his head would be cut off and put on a spear.

Willie believed the Devil and thought he'd have to go to the Devil's house, but he didn't know where he lived and the Devil hadn't told him how to get there.

Well, he started out on Monday morning. He traveled all week, up till Friday evening, asking everybody he met if they knowed where the Devil lived, and none of 'em could tell him. Friday night he got to his brother's. His brother had married and moved away off there. He stayed all night with his brother and his brother noticed he was in trouble some way. So next morning he axed him what was the matter, and Willie told him that he was going to the Devil and axed him if he knowed where he stayed. His brother knowed nothing about the Devil, and he tried to persuade Willie to give up the journey and stay with him, but Willie said no, he had to go or his head would be put on a spear, sure.

So Willie hit out early Saturday morning and about twelve that day as he was going along he looked down under the bank and seed two girls a-swimming in the river. So he thought they might know something about the Devil and he went down and hollered and axed 'em. One of them was awful pretty and she seemed to do all the talking. She told Willie that they was the Devil's daughters. So Willie told her what had happened and he was afeared if he wasn't at the Devil's house by night his head would be on the spear.

So the pretty girl got out a solid gold needle and told Willie to pluck on the point of it three times with his finger and he'd have wings. So Willie plucked on the point of the needle three times and he had wings and him and the girls flew away. They just riz right up like birds and flew away. The girl told him to light out from the Devil's house a piece and come in a-walking.

So Willie done what she said. He lit out and went on up walking and the girls flew right up to the house. Willie seed the Devil setting under a shade tree in front of the house and he went up and spoke to him. The Devil told him to get a seat and that he seed he'd kept his word.

After a while the girl come out and said come to supper. They got up and went in and Willie had never seed sich a table set in all his life. Just ever'thing and anything one could think of. In talking he mentioned God and the very minute he said it ever'thing was gone off the table and there wasn't a thing there but a bowl of dishwater. The Devil just got up and walked out of the house 'thout saying a word. The girl spoke to Willie. She said, "You musn't ever mention God's name. From now on there won't be anything on the table but dishwater, but you can wish for something better as you set down and hit'll be there."

Then the girl told Willie that the Devil meant to kill him—"All he wants is a good excuse for putting you out of the way." She said the room he'd be put in to sleep had a spear bed in it. That was a bed with sharp spears under it sticking up and when he laid down on it they'd push up through and kill him. "But," the girl told him, "when you go to get in the bed just wish for something better and you'll have a good bed." So Willie done like she'd told him and he had a good bed and slept well and the next morning he was setting before the fire chawing terbacker when the Devil come in. The Devil told him he was going away that day and that his great-grandmother's granny had lost her solid gold ring in the well one time and he wanted him to draw out the water and get it that day, and if he didn't have it when he come in that his head would go on a spear.

So Willie went out and found the well about one-third full of water. He got a bucket and started drawing, but the more he drawed out the fuller hit got and by the time the girl come and said dinner was ready the well was running over. He said no, he couldn't come to no dinner then, for he had to get that water out and find that ring or his head would be on on the spear that night, sure.

She told him to come on and eat his dinner and after dinner she'd go back and help him. So he went on in and there wasn't anything on the table but a bowl of dishwater, but he wished for something better and the table was just loaded with all sorts of good things. So after dinner the girl went back with him to the well and she took a little solid gold dipper and dipped out three dipperfuls and the well was empty and Willie clumb down and found the ring. And that night he give it to the Devil and he took it without a word.

The next morning the Devil started off and told Willie that his great-grandmother's granny lost her thimble in the stable a long time ago and he wanted him to throw out the litter and find hit that day and if he didn't by the time he come in that night his head would go on the spear. So Willie took a shovel and went out to the stable. Wasn't much litter in the stable and he set in shoveling it out, but the more he shoveled the more there was, and by the time the girl come out and told him to come to dinner, the stable was running over with litter. He told the girl he couldn't possibly come to dinner, for if he didn't find the thimble by night his head would be on the spear sure. But she told him to come on and she'd go back and help him after dinner. So he went on and ate and after dinner she took a little solid shovel and went with him. She just shoveled three shovelfuls and the stable was as clean as your hand. And they looked around and found the thimble and that night when the Devil come in Willie handed it to him. He took it without saying a word.

The third morning when the Devil started off he took Willie down below the house and showed him a big flat rock. He said that he wanted a big two-story house with twenty-four rooms built on that big rock and that he wanted it built of stone and furnished ready to live in

103

that night, and if it wasn't ready his head would go on the spear. Willie didn't know what to do, but he got an old rock axe and started in, but the more he worked the bigger the stone got and when the girl called him to dinner he didn't have as much as one stone ready. He told her no, that he couldn't come, that if he didn't have that house built by night his head would sure be on the spear. She told him to come on and eat and she'd go back with him after dinner and help him some. So he went on an eat dinner and after dinner the girl got a little solid gold axe and went back with him and struck on the flat rock three times and there stood a two-story house with twenty-four rooms all ready to live in. Now, she told Willie, when the Devil comes in tonight you show him the house and he'll like it, but after he starts on, you fall back fifteen steps and the house will disappear.

So that evening when the Devil come in Willie took him through the house and he was well pleased with it. The Devil started on to supper and Willie stopped till he was fifteen steps ahead of him and called the Devil and they looked back and the house was gone. No sign of it. The Devil was mad, but Willie told him that he said build the house. He hadn't said anything about letting hit stand.

The next morning the Devil went off, but he didn't say anything about Willie doing anything that day. He hadn't been gone but a little while till the girl told Willie to go to the stable and catch the poorest horse and the poorest mule he could find and bring them down to the stile block in front of the house and they'd go and get married. Willie was right in for that. So he done what she said. Got out to the stable and there stood the poorest, boniest mule you ever seed and a horse that was a good match for him. So he bridled 'em and led them down to the stile block and the girl come out and throwed a saddle on the mule and he was the fattest finest mule he'd ever laid eyes on, and just raring and pitching he was so full of life, and when she saddled the hoss he was the same way.

So the girl got on the mule and told Willie to get on the hoss and away they went. Went on about a half a day and Willie looked back and seed the Devil a-coming just as hard as he could tear. The girl told Willie to jump off his hoss and get a gravel and put it in her mule's ear. He did and all at once all behind them was just big rocks, cliffs and boulders. The Devil had to go back and get tools to move 'em with and they got another start on him. But after while Willie looked back and seed him coming again. The girl told Willie to jump off his hoss and pick a thorn and put it in her mule's ear. He did and all at once all behind them was the awfulest thorn thicket they had ever seed. So the Devil had to stop and go back and go back to git tools to cut 'em down with and they got a right smart start on him again. But after a while Willie looked back and seed him a-coming. The girl told him to jump down and take her thimble and dip it up full of water and dash it in her mule's ear. Willie done what she told him and all at once the country they'd passed through was a sea of water. The Devil didn't like water and he turned back. They went on and got married and went back and took possession of ever'thing. The Devil never showed up, and the last time I heard of Willie and that girl, they was a-getting along pretty well.

## Sampson and the Devil

*This tale was collected by Richard Chase, then of Damascus, Virginia, from Jesse Johnson of Wise County, Virginia, in 1941 or 1942, February 9, 1948. Courtesy of Ben Heiman,*

*Huntsville, Alabama, and obtained from the collection of Ferrum College, Ferrum, Virginia.*

One time Sampson and the Devil got to trying to outdo each other. They wrestled but neither one could throw the other. They tried toting logs but Sampson could get as many up on his shoulders as the Devil could. They lifted bulls but every bull the Devil got off of the ground Sampson could do it too. Till finally the Devil said, "I've got a hammer down yonder, Sampson, and if you can throw my hammer as high as I can we'll stand off. We'll just quit and I'll admit that you're as good a man as I am. You ain't really outdone me yet, and I don't think you ever will."

Sampson said all right, so the Devil went and got his hammer.

They got in a field and everybody stood around to see the Devil throw his hammer. So the Devil whirled his hammer and let it go. It went up out of sight. They all kept looking up for it to fall but it didn't, so the Devil looked around and sort of grinned at Sampson, says, "No use waiting around. I'll just tell ye now. You all come back about twelve tomorrow. It'll take about that long for it to fall back down."

So next day everybody came back and got around that field and about one o'clock here came that hammer. Wham! Hit the ground and mired about three feet past

the handle. Then the Devil reached down and pulled it out, laid it there on the ground.

"All right, Sampson. Now you throw it."

Sampson walked out in the field and walked up one side of the hammer, walked around the head of it, looking it over, and here he came walking back to the end of the handle. Everybody was watching Sampson and the old Devil stood there with one hand in his pocket and grinning like a bobcat.

Sampson rolled up one sleeve, spit on his hands, laid hold on the handle, and then he looked way up in the sky and hollered, "Hey, Gabriel! Stand back way over on one side! Hey, you, Saint Peter! Get that gate wide open and run back out the way, quick!"

The Devil quit grinning right off.

"Hold on, Sampson," he says, "I don't want it pitched that high—not up there. I had to leave that place in a hurry once, and if my hammer was to land in there I never would get it back."

The Devil took up his hammer and he left—went on home.

### Jack and the Devil

*This is another tale collected by James Taylor Adams from Gaines Kilgore of Wise, Virginia, on November 23, 1941. He had heard his father tell it. From the James Taylor Adams papers, John Cook Wyllie Library, Clinch Valley College, Wise, Virginia. Courtesy of Robin Benke. See Charles L. Perdue's* Outwitting the Devil: Jack Tales From Wise County, Virginia *(Santa Fe: Ancient City Press, 1987).*

One time there was a boy named Jack. Jack was a poor boy, but he saved a few pennies now and then until by the time he was twenty-one and free he had a hundred dollars saved up. So he started out to seek his fortune and find something to invest his money in.

So Jack went on and on until one day he was going down the road when he met up with the Devil.

"Where you going, Jack?" said the Devil.

"Oh, I'm just going out to seek my fortune and find something to invest my money in," said Jack.

"Well," said the Devil, "I've got a hundred dollars too. Why don't we put our money together and go into business?"

"That'd suit me exactly," said Jack.

So Jack and the Devil put their money together and then begin to consider what they'd go in to.

"There orta be good money in farming," said the Devil. "Let's raise corn. You know people have to have corn."

"All right," said Jack. "That suits me."

So they got 'em some land and planted a big field of corn. Oh, it growed off just fine, and before it was time to gather it the Devil said, "Now we'll have to out some way to divide our crop. Tell you what I'll do, Jack, I'll take what grows under the ground and you can have what grows on top. You see, I'm sort of an underground feller anyhow."

"All right," said Jack, "that suits me."

So that fall when they gathered their crop Jack got all the corn and fodder and the Devil got nothing but the

roots. But he was a game feller and took it without any kick.

The next year they decided to raise taters. Before time to gather 'em the Devil said he believed he would take what growed on top of the ground. So they agreed that way, and when they dug the taters Jack got all the taters and the Devil had nothing left but the tops. But he was a game sort of feller and raised no kick about it.

So the next year they agreed to go into the hog-raising business. They got a whole lot of sows and a few boars and let 'em loose in a big field. Oh, they growed off fine and they brought pigs, and hit wasn't long till the field was plum full of fine hogs.

Now the Devil was running short of money and he said they'd have to divide the hogs so he could sell his share and have money to start again on. So they figured out a way to divide 'em. They agreed to git in the field and each one could have the hogs he could catch and throw over the fence in another joining field. That's what they done. Oh, it took 'em two or three days to catch and throw 'em all over. But at last they had 'em all throwed over and neither one of 'em could figure or count so they had no way of telling which hogs each one had throwed over. So they didn't know how they'd ever tell their hogs apart. Jack had an idea, and said, "Look here, ever' hog I throwed over I jerked a quile in his tail." So they got over and looked and ever' hog had a quile in his tail.